Who
Stole my
Joy?

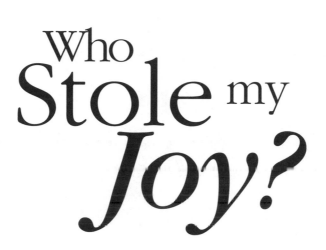

Who Stole my Joy?

Uncover the *Joy Robbers* of Your
Present Circumstance and
Discover the *Joy Builders* of Your Best Life

by Sandra Steen

Bridge-Logos
Orlando, Florida 32822

Bridge-Logos

Orlando, FL 32822 USA

Who Stole My Joy?
by Sandra Steen

Copyright ©2007 by Bridge-Logos

Printed in the United States of America.

Library of Congress Catalog Card Number: 2006937518
International Standard Book Number: 0-88270-343-9, 978-0-88270-343-5

Scripture quotations in this book are from the *King James Version* of the Bible.

G163.316.N.m701.35250

Dedication

This book is dedicated to God Almighty,
the Author, the Finisher, and the Creator of *Joy*.
Thank you for the joy You bring!

Contents

Introduction

Tears of Joy, Tears of Sorrow

The tears of joy and the tears of sorrow
flow from the same eyes, but from different minds.
—*Sandra Steen*

The sun was so sweet and warm as it hugged the earth on that particularly beautiful summer day. I had been up for hours most of the night before, planning a presentation for my next speaking event. Preparation for these engagements has always been an intense exercise for me. I would command from myself the proper attitude so that no matter what the subject, I would be able to deliver it with joy and delight my audiences.

Sometimes, however, the circumstances of the day would not oblige, making it difficult for me to feel the proper emotional energy needed to thrill an audience. Whenever this happened, thrilling my audience and bringing joy to their lives was anything but easy. In fact, I had begun to notice that it always seemed to be just before "show time" that I would undergo some of life's big and little attacks. It amazed me that, in spite of receiving bad news, I could still find joy and carry on. Anybody can be joyful when everything is perfect, I realized. However, when life's big and little attacks ambushed me, usually just moments before approaching the podium, my need to hold on to joy's encouragement and strength was palpable.

The worst time, the worst of life's big attacks, came the night of that particularly beautiful and warm summer day. I was scheduled for two speaking engagements and one television appearance, all on the same day. This was somewhat unusual, because normally my staff was sensitive about not overcrowding my calendar. I had agreed to the challenging schedule and had been up most of the night preparing for the three engagements. Little did I know that on this busiest of all days I would receive the worst news possible! Life's attack came around 1 a.m. It was my brother calling, and I could barely understand what he was saying. His voice, twisted and gnarled with emotion, was letting me know that our mother had died. The sense of loss I felt at that moment took me to profound depths of sorrow and despair. At that moment, I felt like a three-year-old girl, lost in a mall and looking for her mother, only to find that she was gone forever. The grief thrust upon me from losing my mother was as deep as it was indescribable.

I have always been known for telling my audiences that when you don't feel the part, act the part and you will become the part—or, as I would rephrase it, "Fake it until you make it, Baby." On that day, those words would come home; I knew the emotion I was feeling certainly was not joy. After all, the word joy means "gladness of heart, delight, or a sense of well-being." Who could feel those at a time like this? Would I be able to fake it through three speaking engagements?

When I arrived at the hospital at about 2 A.M., I saw all of my family members standing sadly around my mother's lifeless body. Immediately stepping into "business mode," just as everyone expected me to, I started making the necessary arrangements. Numbed and grief-stricken, I was not in touch with my feelings, yet I knew I had things to do. I told my family that I was going to cancel all of my engagements for that day, because I knew it would be too difficult for them to follow through. My family surprised me by disagreeing. They told me that it was precisely on a day such as this that I could truly bring something special to my audiences. At first, I hesitated. But with their encouragement, I decided that maybe this is what I should do after all. I had spoken with my mother just the night before, and she had told me she would be watching the show. I decided this would be a great tribute to her.

My first assignment was at 9 A.M. I was scheduled to participate in a television talk show, the subject of which had been planned weeks ago. Ironically, my discussion topic was "Dealing with Difficult Situations." Somehow, I made it through the 10-minute segment, during which I told the audience of my news. Suddenly, calls began to come in from listeners who said they could not believe my strength and that they would never forget this day. They somehow found the answers to their own difficult situations just by my showing up despite the hours-young loss of my mother. I made it through the show without shedding a tear, and I actually managed to smile, as usual. I saw tears in the eyes of the talk show host and some of the show's staff members, who showed understanding and appreciation because I had kept my commitment to them.

The day's second engagement was a lunch meeting with a women's group at an exclusive country club. I had prepared a specific topic for this event; however, I ended up changing my message and talking to this group of women about living life with joy. I used my mother as an example: in spite of her pain, I saw and heard her singing and encouraging us even as she lay suffering on her sickbed. It comes back to me in a blur sometimes, but I do remember the tears at this luncheon event, the women reflecting on things they always took for granted, and how they sometimes misplaced the joy in their own lives.

By the third engagement in the evening, I was physically tired but felt strengthened by the positive experiences during my first two events. This was one of the worst days in my life, but I could still bring joy to my audiences. The event was a sales conference, and all of the attendees were ready for the excitement of the evening. My reputation for dynamic, lively presentations must have preceded me, because everyone was eagerly looking forward to it. This time, however, I did not share my news with the audience. I attempted to give them the original message I had prepared, and I pulled myself together so that they could leave energized, vibrant and lively, with their expectations fully met. According to the audience response, it worked—everyone was "pumped."

Of course, during the days after those engagements ended and the finality of my mother's passing had come, I experienced my moments of grief and disappointment. Nevertheless, working through these difficulties, I learned that we don't have to give up our "gladness of heart." I realized how important joy is to the overall process of living. I also realized how disposable joy becomes when life brings on its challenges. I can also remember times in my life without joy, and I remember what a dark place that can be. Joy became a precious gift for me, and I decided I didn't want to ever give it up.

My grandmother used to say, "There's always something to take the joy out of living." These words seemed all too true to me, but I determined in my mind and my spirit that, indeed, I would fight to keep my joy. At times, someone would challenge me by doing something incredibly aggravating or saying something dreadfully rude. I realized I could respond with firmness, but at the end of the transaction, I could not leave my joy on their counter. I understood how costly this would be.

As I write this now, it has been four years since the day of my mother's passing. As bad as that day seemed, I have had far too many days that have tried to compete with its grief and emptiness. At the end of those days, I have found that I can still wake up the next morning renewed in my heart, mind, and spirit. I know that weeping will accompany me during the night, but joy will soothe my cheek in the morning. For this reason, I have written this book in the hope that life's "joy robbers" will be exposed and prevented from operating so freely to destroy our spirit.

I hope that you will derive benefit from *Who Stole My Joy?* and share it with someone you know. Most of all, I hope that you will learn something in this book that will safeguard your joy for the rest of your life.

1

THE DREAM:

Joy Meets *Lack*

The important things in life are not things at all.
—David Benjamin

I had been in the office the entire morning and afternoon of a particularly stressful day. One thing after another had seemed to leap out at me from the halls, the walls, from the windows and the filing cabinets: an indispensable employee called in sick, my computer crashed, and I broke a nail. Why not throw everything else in, too? There were problems with mail pick-up and delivery, the telephone rang incessantly, loudly and intrusively—all the usual sorts of events that had me wondering if I should have even gotten out of bed that day.

Finally, with the proverbial fires almost out, the monsters killed, and the rats sent packing, I picked up the telephone if only to halt its nonstop ringing. I should have left it trilling and twisting its way through digital limbo. I could not believe what I was hearing. This was not the first, not the second, but the third call of its kind this week. An important client had an unexpected change of plans: a budget cut had occurred, and a substantial amount of business with my company had been cut with it. The message was all too clear: "No more work, we're sorry, Ms. Steen."

I immediately began to panic about what these three cancellations would mean for our cash flow and my company's future. How would we meet all of our financial obligations without this planned revenue? At least there were some options, kind of like choosing whether to have gastric bypass surgery or have my jaws wired shut. Perhaps I would need to cut some of the staff positions immediately. Or I could evaluate what personal lifestyle changes I would have to make. Another option was to pursue other ways to make money.

This was a terrible moment. Insecurity seemed to take on a live form, invading my every thought. One thing was certain: planning to "live with *Lack*" would not be easy or joyful. It was obvious to everyone around me that my usual joyous demeanor had been overtaken by heartache, sadness, and an almost paralyzing fear of the future.

I decided the stress was too much. I needed to go home and evaluate the choices I would need to consider in order to deal with the huge gap that had just been created in my financial future. This would be a good time to reflect and meditate. I would add this situation to my prayer list.

I remembered that I already had a number of requests on my daily prayer list, and some of these had been on the list for at least five years. I wondered if this situation would also be long term. This recent development should go to the top of the list, I thought, and I should begin immediately working on a good plan while praying fervently.

As I reflected on these recent business losses, I began to take inventory of what was missing in my life. It now appeared to me that life was not producing enough money, time, or fulfillment. This clearly fell into a category I called "*Lack*." I wondered how strong *Lack* could be, because I had adopted the belief that my *Joy* could endure any trial. After all, I had made this commitment to myself that I would not allow my joy to be sacrificed during the "seasons of life." I really wanted to believe that this bad news would pass and *Joy* would remain.

As my reflections played out in front of me, I took a wrong turn emotionally. I arrived and then stayed in a place of dispirited focus:

my thoughts took me again and again to what was missing, broken, incomplete, or simply not there. I could literally feel my joy fading, and I felt emotionally drained as I examined the feeling of deprivation that hovered just outside my door. That night, I cried myself to sleep as I lay in a cold pool of my own tears. But I remember that as I fell into a deep sleep, I had a vivid dream.

In my dream, this particular character with a lifelike presence appeared to me. However, despite his realistic presence, he seemed to be shadowed by an overall demeanor that was suspect. The character introduced himself to me, saying his name was *Lack*.

"I will serve as your *Insufficiency*," he said. "Generally speaking, I don't coexist with *Joy*. I'm a *Circumstance of Life*, and I find myself busy most of the time. I've read in your profile that you are committed to keeping your *Joy* even in the midst of bad circumstances. Sorry, but when I show up, I expect *Joy* to leave, and your joy is no exception."

In my dream, I was speechless. I struggled to respond, but couldn't. Yet I could feel my resistance surging from within. This fellow had some nerve! He was trying to muscle his way into my life and replace my joy and contentment with his discontented, surly self. Oh, how I struggled to surface from this dream and kick *Lack* away for a lifetime!

But the dream continued, with *Lack* explaining to me that he would require an inventory of the things that I thought I needed but that I just couldn't quite find or get to. In my dream, I gasped to myself. *Lack* wanted my wish list! "*Lack* is clearly the enemy," I thought to myself in the dream. "I can't give him my wish list and reveal my position. He'd know too much about me! I'd never get rid of him!"

Oblivious to my dream thoughts, *Lack* continued, "My job is rather complex, you know. I have my own reality show, and I make you, my client, the star! I create the reality of what you lack, and for good measure I also bring in a whole cast and crew of out-of-reach images. It's great entertainment watching my clients deal with those images. My reality show technique is a wonderful tool for cultivating a lack of contentment. I'll enjoy watching you constantly reach for something that's just out of your grasp."

I wanted this dream to end. I was agitated, and could sense myself thrashing around in my bed, trying to wake up and get out of *Lack's* reality show. The words were struggling to come out, and finally I could feel my lips parting as I whispered, "I don't know what you're talking about. I can reach anything I want to, as long as I prepare for it and work diligently to achieve it." Then, exhausted, I fell deep into slumber again, but *Lack* was still there.

Lack answered, "Oh, come on, you know what I mean! It's like trying to live your life as if it were your favorite movie, in which everyone gets what they want. Problem is that the movie ends in three hours, but your life continues after those three hours, daily, weekly, monthly, yearly."

He paused and then continued. "When I, *Lack*, am with you, whether I'm real or perceived, I'll take you away from the path to *Joy*. The path *I'll* take you on is never-ending, and you'll continually look for the things that you can never get enough of, which in turn begets my pained offspring, "*Lack of Joy.*"

Lack smiled at the thought of his offspring, and explained, "You can never get enough of what you really don't need. It's like trying to have enough black shoes. You'll just never have enough of them. It just doesn't happen," he said morosely. "My job is to keep you focused on what's missing to keep you from arriving at contentment."

Then as my dream continued, I saw a beautiful cloud that appeared out of nowhere. From this cloud emerged the most magnificent being I had ever seen. His appearance is hard to describe, for although he was much like an ordinary person, his presence and texture were different. His aura radiated around him, engulfing everything, and yet he seemed humble and unassuming at the same time.

At times, he appeared very tall and commanding; at other times, he appeared not very tall at all. In my dream, I stared curiously at him, wanting to know who he was. I could see myself smiling in my sleep, because it was clear to me that his presence had created a peaceful contentment.

As the object of my curiosity approached, he introduced himself to me as *Joy*. "I represent your gladness of heart and sense of well-being. I'm not just a nice smiley face or a naïve attitude. I am your connection to God and the source of your strength."

As with *Lack*, I was again speechless in my dream, but this time it was because I was awestruck and overcome by this wonderful stranger, this magnificent *Joy*. I sensed that I was no longer turning and thrashing in my bed. Now a sweet calm came over me, enfolding me ever so gently in the gossamer silk threads of my bed sheets—which in my waking world were really a cotton/polyester blend.

Joy then took on a stronger presence and became more aggressive with me, telling me I needed to recognize that *Lack* was simply trying to displace him in my life.

"*Lack* is a *Joy Robber*," he said, "here to steal from you your contentment and gladness of heart. Your thinking and your focus is the best anti-theft device you can use to prevent this from happening." *Joy's* voice became louder. "I won't leave unless you tell me to go. The choice is yours to make. Remember that while you may not have everything that you desire, you don't have to lose your joy."

"I don't want to lose you," I replied. Suddenly, I didn't have to struggle to speak.

Then *Joy* smiled serenely, saying: "You have given me a permanent place in your life based on your own personal confession. You have made a commitment to allow me to coexist with the *Circumstances of Life*."

As my dream continued, I replied: "Right now I'm finding that commitment easier said than done. I have issues that I don't understand."

Joy's voice became more powerful, yet more comforting. "Anybody can find *Joy* when life is providing your every desire. But now is the most important time to find joy, when life is dealing you what can appear as an unfair circumstance." He looked at me with intensity and lowered his voice. "I am here for you," he said.

The dream continued. *Joy* began to tell me:

"Nothing missing and nothing broken is not based on what is in your inventory; it is based on a state of mind. It is the basis of Peace. When the right things are in place, you don't need to look around for the things that are not needed. Whatever you choose to focus on will take on size."

I began to smile again and found myself transformed by my mind's renewal. I told *Joy* I had experienced a temporary loss of self, but I was back and he should stay.

Lack sat there quietly during this entire conversation. He then spoke to *Joy* and said, "Well, you might have won here, but I know of some places that you won't be allowed. In fact, I happen to know both *Circumstances of Life* and *Emotional Issues.* Each is a stand-up *Joy Robber,*" *Lack* chortled, "and you could never coexist with them, *Joy.*"

Joy responded, "So you happen to know some of those other *Joy Robbers.* So what? I happen to have an idea. Since I need a stronger voice to be able to expose your gang of thieves, my group, the *Joy Builders,* is going to go on an expansion project. I promise you that through this project, the invisible will become visible, and the joy robbing will stop."

In a commanding yet kind manner, *Joy* continued, telling us that his plan was to meet with all the *Joy Robbers* and find out what makes them successful with their clients. "You know that knowledge is powerful, and without knowledge you can be destroyed," *Joy* said. "So in order to stop the joy robbing, I must have information and then seek to change the situation. I don't want any of my clients to find that their *Joy* has been stolen. My idea is to help those who have lost their *Joy* to find it."

Joy then told us that he would also meet with some of his strong partners, among them *Positive Attitude* and *Hope.* He would ensure that they continue supporting him. During his journey, *Joy* told us, he would find out whom he could coexist with and whom he could replace.

Joy continued, "I know this is an aggressive campaign, but if I don't make the attempt, there will be a lot of people walking around without me—you see, I bring them 'gladness of heart.' I must find them before *Lack* and all the *Joy Robbers* have them thinking that I don't exist. I believe that I can help make this a better world, and I intend to go near and far to find the answers I need. By the way, *Lack,* before I start on my journey I want to ask you for your client list. I will make sure that whenever you appear, I will be there to make sure you do not destroy your client's *Joy.*"

Lack agreed, since he had firsthand experience with how aggressive *Joy* could get and he did not want a confrontation. *Lack* made a mental note to himself that *Joy* had a lot more energy than he did. *Joy* then said that he had to move on, because he had lots of work and he wanted to get some rest. The next day he was meeting with *Broken Relationships,* and he knew that this *Circumstance of Life* had affected many of his clients.

Joy spoke directly to me and said, "When I complete this process, I know you will have found the answers you and many others need to always keep me around."

I nodded, because somehow I knew that while *Joy* was on this important mission, he would never leave me. I smiled knowing that *Joy* had earned a permanent place in my life.

2

Joy Meets *Broken Relationships*

All relationships start and end in the mirror.
— *Sandra Steen*

Thus, *Joy* begins his journey to coexist with the *Circumstances of Life*. He meets what he has been told would be one of his strongest opponents, *Broken Relationships*.

Joy met *Broken Relationships* in the hallways of the divorce courts. It appeared no one seemed happy here. *Broken Relationships* introduced himself to *Joy* and explained that he was the "granddaddy" of all the *Joy Robbers,* because no one wins. Everyone comes out of the situation with the loss of their *Joy*. *Broken Relationships* continued by telling *Joy* that his influence is felt in all kinds of associations, whether it is between spouses, or among family members or friends. When *Joy* responded that he wanted to spend time working with *Broken Relationships,* the idea was met with ridicule, and *Broken Relationships* walked away from *Joy* with an arrogant air.

Joy stood quietly for a moment as *Broken Relationships* turned his back on him, and then he yelled, "Wait one minute! You didn't steal *Joy*! *Failed Expectations* did, so why are you taking the credit for stealing anyone's *Joy*?"

Broken Relationships turned. He pushed his way back down the hall towards *Joy*, past the children who wept, the spouses who fought, and the clandestine lovers who laughed (but not for long). "It really doesn't matter," he answered, "if I take the credit or if *Failed Expectations* claims it. The bottom line is that when I show up, you leave, Mr. '*Joy* to the World.'" *Broken Relationships* laughed smugly and continued, "It will always happen that way—I guarantee it."

Joy reached into his pocket and began to look at notes he had prepared for this visit. Gazing back at him steadily, *Joy* responded, "I am absolutely certain that I really can stay around with you despite what you are saying, Mr. *Broken Relationships,* and that I don't need to leave. Since you are so confident that I can't stay, then tell me why you think your clients sign up with you in the first place!"

Broken Relationships sighed impatiently. "Every relationship begins in the mirror," he told *Joy,* "but all broken relationships look at someone else's reflection other than their own. My clients love to play the blame game on each other. In many cases, my clients always want to believe they are right, even if that means they are not reconciled in their relationship. In the case of a broken relationship, they must decide if they want to be right or reconciled. If that's not happening, then someone is bearing the burden of guilt for the failed relationship. It's a vicious cycle."

On a roll now, *Broken Relationships* told *Joy* that some of the other *Joy Robbers* had sent lots of business his way: *Joy Robbers* such as *Selfishness, Insecurity,* and *Jealousy*, just to name a few.

"And my list of referrals goes on!" he bragged to *Joy.* "The bottom line," he explained, "is that I will always be in business because it is my job to make sure that my clients do not honor their *Commitment* to one another. My clients believe that a *Commitment* is merely an option, and that *Unconditional Love* is available whenever it is convenient. My clients often interpret *Love* as a physical feeling rather than a *Choice.* As a *Broken Relationship*, I realize I am not an *Emotion*, but a *Circumstance of Life,* and I am here to stay."

Suddenly introspective, *Broken Relationships* told *Joy* that it is amazing how all of his clients start their relationships on such a strong and positive note. "It's equally amazing," he continued, "how all of my clients end their relationships on such a negative note."

Thinking aloud, *Broken Relationships* continued, "You know, I could actually lose a lot of clients if they commit to each other to 'end positive,' no matter what happens. I've noticed that I don't seem to get clients who understand how to work their relationships vertically with God as well as horizontally with the person."

Joy smiled and replied, "I have some important information for you. If you can envision that when you work a relationship vertically with God and horizontally with the person, the image you see is a cross, which is the symbol of unconditional love. Have you ever noticed that?"

"Now that you mention it…" *Broken Relationships* replied, pausing momentarily to gather his thoughts. Then he quickly continued, "Of course, if my clients understood that image and applied unconditional love, I would have very few clients left."

Now *Broken Relationships* stopped talking. "Me and my big mouth," he thought to himself. He realized that he'd perhaps gone beyond what he should have revealed. After all, he was not trying to equip *Joy* with too much valuable information. "Oh well," he thought, "most folks don't understand that concept, anyway."

Intrigued, *Joy* told *Broken Relationships* that he wasn't intending to replace him, as that would be almost impossible, but he was wondering how they could work together. *Broken Relationships* answered, "If you want to work with my clients, you need to create a *Joy* that can overcome *Bad Circumstances*, because that's what I am." *Broken Relationships* looked at his watch because he knew a broken relationship was happening just about every minute, and he didn't have time to talk any more with *Joy*. He walked away to work with clients at a divorce hearing.

Gazing thoughtfully at *Broken Relationships* hurrying into a nearby courtroom, *Joy* now realized that creating a sense of well-being during a time of personal loss is not an easy task. After this interesting exchange, however, he was now looking forward to working with *Broken Relationships'* clients.

A child passed him, covering her ears with her hands as she walked between her two angry and screaming parents. They hovered over her like fighter helicopters, pointing their fingers at one another and flailing their arms in the dense air above her head. *Joy* reached down to dry her tears and softly whispered, "Dear one, I can't wait to spend some time with you."

3

Joy Meets *Jealousy*

In jealousy, there is more of self-love than love.
—*François de la Rochefoucauld*

When *Joy* met *Jealousy,* he felt somewhat leery of him because *Jealousy* appeared not to have very much presence. *Jealousy* almost seemed not to even be there, an ephemeral presence, as if he were in hiding, trying not to be seen.

Jealousy introduced himself and told *Joy* that in his experience, only *False Joy* could coexist with him; no virtue or emotion, no blessed beatitude could replace him. Telling *Joy* that sometimes people don't even realize he is there, *Jealousy* explained that once he makes it clear that he has arrived, his clients generally go into denial.

"Your comment about *False Joy* interests me, *Jealousy,*" *Joy* responded. Continuing, he said, "As *True Joy,* I need to understand my own position relative to yours a little better. I'm wondering if you and I really can coexist, despite your opinion to the contrary. I hope you'll let me ask you some questions about your job responsibilities."

With uncharacteristic generosity and openness, *Jealousy* agreed to the interview.

"Why are you so busy?" *Joy* began.

Jealousy answered that he appears when a comparison takes place: "If my clients did not compare themselves to each other, I would be out of a job. Have you heard the old proverb that says the grass always looks greener on the other side?"

Without waiting for *Joy* to answer, *Jealousy* continued, "My clients will not consider the possibility that the neighbors on the other side of that fence choose to pay a great deal more attention to their grass. For example, by using more water, buying or making compost, and even paying a higher water bill, the person who owns the grass on the other side of the fence has a prettier lawn.

"What I do is deceive my clients into thinking they do not have equal access to the water and fertilizer for any number of reasons: unfair enterprise, bad luck, etc."

Jealousy paused and added rhetorically: "Do you think maybe this is why people call me 'The Green-eyed Monster?'"

"You know," *Jealousy* continued, switching subjects, "I get a lot of work because people do not understand the concept of timing or seasons."

Joy's curiosity was aroused. "I don't think I've heard of that concept." He asked what *Jealousy* meant by that and why it would be important to understand.

"You see, the seasons of a person's life are constantly evolving. If you compare your winter to another person's summer, you will most likely become resentfully envious. However, when you know your winter is changing, you are able to develop a different perspective," *Jealousy* replied.

Joy wanted to find out from *Jealousy* what it would take to replace him, and *Jealousy*, in an unusual gesture again, seemed almost eager to share. He started out by telling *Joy* that his clients usually begin in the harmless state initiated by his little stepbrother, *Jealous Nudge*.

"*Nudgie* just keeps them on their toes, is all," *Jealousy* explained. After seeing someone else's success, he merely prompts my clients to wish that success would happen for them."

Jealousy continued explaining. "After playing with *Jealous Nudge* for a while, my clients move on to our stepsister, *Jealous Anger*. She helps them build an angry resentment against the person whom they believe is purposely and unfairly exceeding their level, their bank account, the size of their house, or whatever."

"Really! What a sad waste of energy and emotion!" exclaimed *Joy*.

"That's not all," continued *Jealousy*. "The next stage is when my clients judge the person they are jealous of. They start believing that this person does not deserve their success. This leads my clients to one of my most dangerous relatives, *Jealous Sabotage*, and sometimes, even *Murder*, the most dangerous of all my relatives. When this happens, my family gathers with the full force of its irrational and negative energies. Together they coerce my clients to hinder the success of the individuals that they envy.

"In some extreme cases, my nastiest relatives have succeeded in convincing my clients to bring harm to the person. This, of course, is the extreme stage. If my clients don't take time out for intervention during the first stage, they could advance to the final stage with my entire *Jealous* family, bringing harm to themselves and others." Shrugging, *Jealousy* added: "But most of my clients are silent about our partnership, so they don't usually get help, which only complicates the matter."

Now *Joy* smiled, because he knew that *Jealousy* had unwittingly given him the answer to his question: the two cannot coexist, as *Joy* initially had hoped. But *Joy* could certainly replace him. *Jealousy* looked at *Joy* and wondered what he had up his sleeve. Feeling overworked and underpaid when compared to the other *Joy Robbers*, *Jealousy* really wanted to be out of a job. He hoped that *Joy* had plans to replace him.

"That *Joy* is so lucky to have a job like his. He gets to travel and everything," *Jealousy* whined to himself. "I should have those perks, not him! I'm the one who drums up a whole lot more intense energy in my clients—I work much harder than he does! It's not fair!"

4

Joy Meets *Negative Attitude*

Believing only the negative is deception.
Believing only the positive is "work."
—*Sandra Steen*

When *Joy* met *Negative Attitude*, the vibes were clear: "Everyone has an occasional bad day," *Negative Attitude* said glumly. "Sometimes people also work up a negative attitude to go with it. Some folks hang around with me for just that occasional bad day—others have signed a lifetime contract with me." Sourly, he continued: "You can't expect me to go away, because that would be too unrealistic. Believe it or not, some folks think they like me."

Joy, nonplused for a brief moment, managed to answer lightly: "You must mean some folks are happy when they're mad, and glad when they're sad." He smiled brightly at *Negative Attitude*.

"Smart-guy, aren't you?" was the testy reply. "Frankly," *Negative Attitude* continued, "you can coexist with me only when I allow it. I call the shots. My clients can be negative whenever and however they feel. When they choose a negative attitude, you will not be allowed to hang around with us. The days they're okay, however, you can stay with them until they feel the need for change."

Joy said to *Negative Attitude*, "It looks as if I can't coexist with you. What I really need to do is replace you."

Negative Attitude looked at him and smirked: "Who do you think you are? No one wants to be happily joyful all the time! I need to balance people's lives and provide options for them to choose from. With me around, they can choose to feel mean and morose, grim and ghastly. For some folks, that's normal. For many of my clients, 'keeping it real' and being 'real' means being negative."

Joy replied that what is needed is not a balance of the negative and the positive, but a continuous fight to remain positive. "Don't you see, *Negative Attitude,* that whenever you show up, these people lose their productivity and zest for life and love? In fact," *Joy* continued pointedly, "you've created some of the other *Joy Robbers* I ran into earlier today. I just came from a meeting with your pal, *Broken Relationships.* I'm sure everyone sets out to have one of those!"

Joy went on with more accusations, explaining that *Negative Attitude* has spawned the harmful toxins of *Mean Words,* causing the mouths of his clients to speak *Death* rather than *Life.* "You're going to have a lot of very sick clients after a while, because they're all going to be full of your poison."

Negative Attitude answered, "I do hear what you are saying, you big crybaby bleeding heart, but I'm just doing my job, man. I have effectively created the downfall of companies and relationships all over the world. What more can I say? I'm rotten because I'm supposed to be!"

Joy looked at *Negative Attitude,* amazed at the depth of meanness in his spirit. "Tell me what you think would put you out of business," *Joy* prompted.

Negative Attitude shook his head and said: "Oh, *Joy,* you sly rascal, you. Now you want trade secrets. You know you really are a demanding little guy."

Joy replied, "Well, let me put it to you this way, *Negative Attitude.* I am not leaving until I find a way to work with your clients, so you might as well cooperate or you are going to have a very long day."

"All right, all right! I'll tell you what would put me out of business," *Negative Attitude* replied. "If my clients could learn to replace their negative thoughts with positive thoughts, that's what.

Most of the time, my clients try to eliminate me, but I'm really an intense sort of guy. I have to be replaced with something positive, but I jealously guard my space. You see what I do is, I hang around in my clients' thought-life, and then my clients become what they think about all day long! You are what you eat, right? With me around, you are what you think!

"If my clients could understand how to capture a positive thought or a terrific idea and make it a reality, I would certainly be out of business. The problem for my clients is that they often fail to realize that what they feed their thoughts over time eventually becomes the life that they live."

At last, *Joy* understood. "Now I get it, *Negative Attitude*," *Joy* replied. "Before you were an attitude, you were a thought. Is that what you're telling me?"

"Correct," responded *Negative Attitude*. "As I continue to shape the thinking of my clients, I am also shaping their character."

"Sounds like you're actually doing too much already," Joy said. "Let me assure you that I will be working hard to get you an early retirement package."

"Oh, that's right! Throw me out in the cold, you ingrate! After all I've taken the time to explain to you, *Joy*, that's all the thanks I get? I'll bet that retirement package will fit inside my mother's sewing thimble," snorted *Negative Attitude*. "Thanks for nothing."

5

Joy Meets *Hopelessness*

There are no hopeless situations;
there are only men who have grown hopeless about them.
—*Clare Boothe Luce*

This time, *Joy* found himself in a dark cave when he met *Hopelessness*. It was so dark he could barely see himself. *Hopelessness* introduced himself as a master of deception. He said he generally darkens every escape route of life and leads his clients to his cave, where they give in to some of their most despairing thoughts. *Hopelessness* said the interesting thing is that he can affect people from all walks of life, and it does not matter how educated or wealthy they are. All he has to do is just cast his long, grim shadow on their thoughts, until they can no longer see any light of hope.

He told *Joy* that he stays in the cave because he cannot stand lightness, brightness, or optimism. "I hate to tell you this," he said gloomily to *Joy*, "but when I show up, life pretty much discontinues, and I know that the two of us could never coexist."

"How dismal of you," commented *Joy*, trying to show empathy while figuring out how to handle this rather bleak-sounding creature.

Hopelessness went on to explain that he doesn't generally just show up suddenly or overnight. Instead, he gives his clients a series of bad experiences and unmet expectations over a period of time. He even told *Joy* that *Broken Relationships* and *Lack* and some of his other *Joy Robber* friends bring him plenty of referrals.

"When my clients have spent their time with some of the other *Joy Robbers*, then I can really put one over on them and drag them into my cave." *Hopelessness* paused a moment and grabbed his head, as if in terrible pain. "In fact," he continued, "I have some expansion plans because I expect more people to lose *Hope* because they are justifying *Negative Attitudes* as their normal state of being. Their continuing self-imposed distress will give me more ground to cultivate."

Joy lowered his head thoughtfully, knowing he had encountered a challenging *Joy Robber*. However, he also knew that he must find a way to replace the desolation that *Hopelessness* causes. Looking now at *Hopelessness*, *Joy* asked what he thought was his most successful deception campaign.

Hopelessness said, "I always defeat *Love*. No one ever comes to me feeling *Loved*.

After writing this important piece of information in his notebook, *Joy* told *Hopelessness* that the gloomy darkness of the cave had become too much for him, and that he really needed to go, but he appreciated his shedding some light on his function. On the way out, *Joy* pointed out an area in the cave and asked why it seemed so much darker in there than anywhere else.

"That's the corner I send my clients to where they can, without restraint, feel that no one cares about or loves them. Everybody that's in there will agree, and they will all make themselves feel even more *Hopeless*. Big pity party. Cool, huh?"

At this point, *Joy* stopped writing. Disgusted, he threw down his notepad and exclaimed, "I can't stand this kind of deception! You know just as well as I that there is not a person in the world who is not loved. Yours is the cruelest and darkest of deceptions, and I promise you that I am going to do my best to prevent you from pulling this off ever again!"

"How could you possibly stop me?" *Hopelessness* asked.

Joy replied, "I'm going to make sure your clients get the "For God So Loved the World" newsletter, that's how!"

Hopelessness began to shudder and told *Joy* that the light he was bringing was beginning to bother his eyes so he must go. "You need to leave now, *Joy*. All this brightness is killing me."

Joy shook his head. As he crawled through the cave's opening into the brilliant and beautiful daylight, he said, "*Hopelessness*, trust me—I've got special lighting equipment for that corner and for this entire cave, in fact. I am truly looking forward to illuminating this place with every possible beam of light, brilliance, and cheer once I replace you."

"I don't think *Joy* likes me," *Hopelessness* thought to himself glumly. "I'll bet nobody does."

6

Joy Meets *Hatred*

Hatred is one of life's greatest energy leaks.
—*Sandra Steen*

*J*oy knew *Hatred* well from the days of the civil rights movement
in the United States, when he had watched *Hatred* marching with
the Ku Klux Klan. Over the years, he had also spotted *Hatred* working
the killing fields of Asia and Africa. Even before that, *Joy* had seen
Hatred rallying the troops in ancient Rome and Carthage, and then
later marching in Europe with the Nazis. He had also run into *Hatred*
at political rallies; but now he wasn't sure where to find him anymore,
given the current environment of political correctness and code-speak.
Joy realized that to locate, interview, and replace *Hatred,* he'd have
to travel the world like an investigative reporter to find *Hatred's*
whereabouts.

"Just how hard are you really looking?" someone asked *Joy.*
"*Hatred's* lurking everywhere, you know, not just in fanatic religions
or in terrorist groups. He's also hiding inside families, schools,
corporate boardrooms and in organizations of every kind. He's a real
sneak, that one!"

Joy refused to believe this. *Hatred* couldn't possibly be thriving
in families, schools, and companies as a welcomed guest! It was
inconceivable! One day as he was out hunting for *Hatred,* a group of

schoolboys walked by rather noisily. Laughing, shoving, and joking aloud, they were discussing the new kid who had just moved into the neighborhood.

"What a dork!" one of them exclaimed. "I can't stand him!"

"Yeah!" responded another. "Those thick glasses, the weirdo language he uses to talk to his dumb sister. My mom says they're strange people with strange customs from some other country, and that we shouldn't even talk to them. Guess we won't be asking him to join our school team or to go to the church picnic."

Disheartened upon hearing this exchange, *Joy* realized that like charity, hatred often begins at home. He wouldn't have to travel to parts of the world torn apart by war and terrorism to find *Hatred*. Indeed, *Hatred* was hanging right here. The one boy had mentioned his church during his conversation about the foreign child. As *Joy* walked along thinking about this, he realized that there was a church of some kind on almost every corner. In fact, this was true of virtually every city and country he had been to. So *Joy* decided to look to *Religion* to get some insight on how *Hatred* might be operating within the scope of conflicting nations and cultures.

When *Joy* first talked to *Religion*, it was a pleasant meeting—at least at the beginning. He felt comfortable thinking *Hatred* was not hiding there. *Joy* was about to conclude the meeting, when out of curiosity he asked, "*Religion,* why do some of your groups appear to be so internally homogenous? In some of your denominations, it appears they associate only with those who think, talk, or even somewhat look alike. I'm not seeing much diversity. It's almost as if they are social clubs rather than faith groups."

"It's a mystery of faith, my child," *Religion* replied, smiling and folding his hands as if in prayer.

Somewhat put off by this self-serving non-answer, *Joy* rolled his eyes. "You mean you don't really want to discuss it!"

"*Joy*, I don't think that you appreciate that we comprise groups that have exclusive rights and insights when it comes to understanding our moral and social issues," *Religion* replied, patting *Joy's* shoulder.

"People who don't understand issues the way we do simply don't belong in our community."

Astounded and intrigued by this exclusionary explanation, *Joy* now suspected he had found one of *Hatred's* secret pathways to gaining clients. *Joy* was on to him! How clever indeed is *Hatred*, lurking in the halls of *Religion*, *Joy* thought to himself.

"Well, then," *Joy* persisted, "how do you feel about religious groups that believe differently from your particular one?"

"On a personal level, I'm sort of okay with the individuals out there who misdirect themselves by thinking differently," *Religion* replied, "but we know that they are wrong in their beliefs and that we are right. Those less committed to our ideals are weak; those more intense are fanatical, those who stand with us, in unquestioning faith and obedience, are standing for the RIGHT!" *Religion's* smile seemed patronizing.

Joy, astounded again, was at a loss for words. The air was now palpable, thick with the silence that had come between them. Suddenly a loud, earsplitting noise shattered the nervous hush in the room. The clattering, deafening din came from nowhere, and yet it came from everywhere. As they jumped and looked around for the source of the startling noise, the ceiling gave way, and a stranger peered down at them through the dust of plaster and broken beams. Neither *Joy* nor *Religion* knew who he was.

"I'm *Hatred*," the new arrival snarled as he tried to crawl out of the hole he had made in the ceiling. "I've been listening to this whole conversation and couldn't conceal myself any longer. You should know that I've been hiding in *Religion's* quarters for centuries, because it's the best venue for serving my clients. Say there, give me a hand to let me down, will ya?"

"Look what you've let out, *Joy*!" *Religion* said unhappily, wagging his finger at *Joy*. "I've tried to keep *Hatred* suppressed, hidden in our closets, ceilings, and basement, but now he's escaping!"

"Didn't someone once say 'Love thy enemy'? While I would have to say that *Hatred* is certainly hard to love, let's not be too hasty to dismiss him," *Joy* whispered back quickly. "*Hatred* seems ready to tell me what I want to know. I'll be able to figure out how to replace him and his hatefulness from what he tells us now." Then, looking back up at *Hatred*, *Joy* said, "I won't be giving you a hand at anything, but I am interested in what you have to say."

"All right. Be that way. And I have plenty to say," *Hatred* told them as he swung down to the floor. "Fortunately for me, I've mastered the ability to hide behind the pleasant chit-chat and conversations. Most of my clients embrace me because of their differing views on race, religion, or nationality.

"My clients feel they don't need justification to hate. Often their hatred is the legacy of those they admire and trust, and they just never question it. They use me to feel superior to others.

"By the way," *Hatred* continued smugly, "you should know that *Jealousy*, one of my fellow *Joy Robbers*, has produced hatred in many of my clients. Together with the splendid work of *Anger* and another *Joy Robber*, *Insecurity*, you can appreciate their potential for developing a strong, hate-filled client base for me. My clients just love all the drama that comes with my product, hatred. I have a guaranteed place here forever because my clients, much as they love all the drama I bring, prefer to remain hidden."

At this, *Joy* wept. But then, remembering his mission, he quickly shifted to a righteous indignation, knowing he was not the kind that would ever shrink back from this villain. *Hatred*, smiling wickedly, told *Joy* that once he left this meeting he would go into hiding again. "You will never replace me," *Hatred* sneered, "because you won't be able to find me. I've learned the clever art of disguise too well."

"Before you leave, tell me what would move clients away from you," *Joy* said, trying to regain control.

"My clients can't stand people who are different from themselves," *Hatred* began. "If ever they started appreciating or celebrating differences, I would lose them. Of course, it's somewhat ridiculous for a hand to say to a foot, 'Because you are not like me, I have no use for you.' Losing one or the other does nothing but damage to the body to which both are connected and for which they perform equally important functions."

Now a loud whimpering could be heard. It seemed to come from somewhere in the attic. *Hatred* groaned. "There's that little brat, crying again!"

"Dad? Dad? Where are you?" More crying.

"Down here, *Odious*, talking to a couple of *Joy Builders*. Come on down so that you can meet them and know who your enemies are."

"What are you telling that precious child?" *Joy* asked *Hatred* indignantly. "He sounds like he's no more than seven years old, yet here you are saying terrible things to him and filling him with *Bitterness* and *Fear*! What kind of a parent are you, anyway?"

Hatred simply gave *Joy* a withering glare and calling back up to his son hollered, "Bring our little chemistry project down with you and quit yer cryin'!"

"Chemistry project?" *Religion* asked curiously. "A chemistry project here in our church?"

"Sure, I'm teaching little *Odious* how to make hate bombs and other types of explosive ammunition. He needs to learn to carry on our mission of physical and spiritual destruction."

Now a young boy's head appeared in the ceiling hole above them. *Odious* was peering down at them, his face streaked with tears.

"Dad, I had a scary dream."

"So that's why you're crying like a baby?" *Hatred* asked *Odious* impatiently. "Well, I guess you'd better let me hear about it. Come on down, *Odious*. Be careful with our chemistry project!"

Joy didn't know what to be more concerned with now: *Hatred*, with his evil, toxic demeanor; *Odious*, his offspring and heir to *Hatred's* poisons; or the hate bomb they were bringing down from the attic. *Joy* expected to see a junior version of *Hatred*, a brutally ugly little creature, vile in every way, as was his father. Instead, young *Odious* was the picture of childhood perfection: firm cheeks and chin; big, bright, sparkling eyes framed by luxuriant lashes and a strong brow; gleaming hair that shone, even through all the dust from the attic; a full mouth that smiled through the tears to reveal dazzling, sugar-white teeth — and dimples to die for. *Joy* gazed at this beautiful little boy, astonished and at once fearful in the knowledge that Odious would soon turn into the abominating image of his father, his handsome, youthful face twisted, punished by the caustic vapors of unredeemable acrimony.

Odious was still whimpering as *Hatred* helped him down from the attic. Putting their chemistry project down on a nearby table, *Hatred* said, "There now, *Odious*, what was it that scared you in your dream? Stop crying, you great big baby!"

Joy and *Religion* looked at each other and grimaced at the unkind way *Hatred* was addressing the youngster. *Odious* turned and gazed at them balefully, then turned to his father and said, "He was in my dream," pointing at *Joy* and beginning to cry again.

Concerned, *Joy* began to step forward, saying "*Odious*, I'm sorry you were scared of me. That's the last thing I would ever want to do to you."

"Stand back, *Joy!*" *Hatred* barked. "I'll handle this—he's my kid, and I want you to stay away from him! *Odious*, don't go near this one," he continued, glowering and pointing at *Joy*. "He'll go against the things I've taught you."

Joy stopped and said, "Why, *Hatred*, is that the protection of *Love* I'm observing here? It's a little sick and twisted, but I do believe that in some degree you love your boy."

"Nice try, *Joy*," replied *Hatred*, "but this is the perfect time for me to tell little *Odious* what he needs to know about the likes of you and your friends, although, *Religion*, you're not such a problem," he continued, pausing to address *Joy's* companion, "because you've actually helped me in the past, even if you didn't realize it or didn't mean to."

Turning to face *Odious*, *Hatred* took the youngster's little face in his hands saying, "*Odious*, this creature standing here with *Religion* is named *Joy*. We don't like him, and I'm going to tell you why. And when I'm through explaining it to you, then I'll let you play with our chemistry project and use it on him. Won't it be fun to see our hate bomb exploding?"

His tears were drying now. "Yeah, Dad, yeah! Oh, boy!" *Odious* began jumping up and down excitedly, then he turned, and curling his lip, gave *Joy* the nastiest look his face could scrunch up into.

Joy and *Religion* exchanged glances again. Reaching into his pocket, *Joy* took out his cell phone and punched in a number. As he put the phone up to his ear, *Hatred* smirked and said, "Oh, look, *Odious—Joy's* calling the cops on us." Then, pitching his voice into a high falsetto, *Hatred* covered his face, exclaiming facetiously, "Ohhhh! We're so scared!"

Joy smirked back. "No, that's my next call. Right now I'm getting a hold of *Love*. I want her to come over and see your splendid presentation of protection and love for your son." *Love* must have answered then, because Joy turned away slightly and said, "Hi, *Love*, *Joy* here. Fine, thanks. Listen, I'm going to send *Religion* over to your place in my Joy Rider to pick you up and bring you over here to the church. *Hatred's* here with us, and you have to see this: he actually loves his son *Odious*, but he's teaching the boy how to make hate bombs! OK, good, *Religion* will be right over. I am amazed that even *Hatred* has some glimmer of *Love* in him. See you in a bit."

Snapping the phone shut, *Joy* gave *Religion* the car keys and said, "*Odious*, you are about to meet one of the finest examples of God's affection for His creation. Her name is *Love*, and she is God's enduring and everlasting gift to all of us."

"Don't talk to my kid about *Love*," *Hatred* snapped. "I'll be the one to tell him." Whirling *Odious* around to face him, *Hatred* crouched down face-to-face with *Odious* saying, "*Odious*, listen to me. We are *Hatred*, the opposite of *Love*. She may claim to endure, but I will be truthful to you and tell you that as *Hatred*, we sometimes don't last as long because there are some things we can't endure. *Love* is one of those things. So that's why you're learning how to make our hate bombs, so that we can outlast her at all costs."

"But Dad, if *Love* never ends, why are we making these bombs?" asked *Odious*.

"Oh, you're in trouble now, *Hatred*," *Joy* interjected, laughing. "You see, *Odious*, *Love* endures because she hopes all things, and *Hope* is a powerful engine that can deflect any of the hate bombs you and your Daddy try to make."

"*Odious*, get me a vial of fuel, you know, from the ones that *Anger* gave you for your birthday, and get some of the nitro from the chemistry set RIGHT NOW!" *Hatred* screamed. "We'll put a blasting agent together and show this Joy Builder we mean business!"

Odious began crying again. "Dad, you're scaring me!" Tears splashed down his innocent young face.

"You're useless!" *Hatred* said to him contemptuously. Then he strode over to the chemistry set to get the items himself.

Joy, though shocked, was undeterred. "*Odious*," he said, "Not only does *Love* hope all things, she believes all things, and she believes there is *Hope* for you to get past this." Turning to *Hatred*, *Joy* said, "There's not a blasting agent of hatred you can make that *Love* cannot overcome. She can bear all things, even you."

Just then, footsteps could be heard rushing down the hallways and into the room. *Love* had arrived, with *Religion* trailing behind. Her beauty captivated even *Hatred*, who paused in his bomb making a moment to stare at her.

"Dad, I saw her in my scary dream, too, with *Joy*," *Odious* said, pointing at her.

"Yes, *Odious*, *Joy* and I came to you last night in your dream, but it wasn't to scare you, and I'm sorry if we did. We came to bring you not just our own gifts, but the gift of *Hope*, too. We want you to grow up in the peace and contentment of a safe and happy childhood. We get so sad when we see your dad, *Hatred*, do these things that are so wrong. Making hate bombs is wrong, *Odious*."

"I resent the way you're interfering with how I'm raising my kid!" *Hatred* exclaimed, visibly irritated. He began pouring his vile concoction into a blasting cap.

"What? Do I hear any semblance of *Love* for your child, *Hatred*?" *Joy* asked innocently.

"No, you don't," *Hatred* snarled. "I'm just using him to complete my mission."

"Dad, Dad, no!" *Odious* cried even harder than before, his tears now rivers running down his cheeks.

Love, near tears herself, said: "*Odious*, so many misunderstand my gift. Because of the strength of character needed to carry on in *Love's* magnificence, some would choose to label me as wimpy or weak, in order to deny my power; but they are so very wrong. Though it's tough at times to walk with me, I will amaze you, *Odious*, with the rewards I can bring to you."

"Rewards?" asked *Odious*, drying his tears. "But I get such a big bang out of blowing up the hate bombs with my dad. If you don't have hate bombs, too, then why are you so great?"

"The power of my gift is that you'll be able to give it even to those who don't give it back. You see, anyone can exchange a gift of love with someone who will give you love in return. That's just so easy.

"But the true champions and heroes in this world are those who've learned my great secret about the power of love, even if the love is not reciprocated. That's not easy at all. My power, you see, lies in the fact that, even for those who choose not to return it, my love continues through my constant and unwavering will to endure. My gift of enduring love is a power that, though you do not yet know or understand it, will ultimately disarm your hate bombs."

Odious simply looked at *Love*, then crossed his arms and waited for more. *Joy* didn't think *Odious* was buying—at least not yet.

Seeing the doubt in his eyes and the resistance in his body language, *Love* continued gently, "Don't start thinking as *Love* I'm a doormat, a slave, or a wimp, *Odious*. Just understand, as I do and as *Joy* does, that when you sow *Hatred*, it will return and destroy you in the end. That's the difference between me as *Love* and your father as *Hatred*: I survive because I don't throw hate bombs, and I don't sow or reap the seeds of destruction. Instead, I'm a builder and maker of *Life*."

"Well, why isn't it easy to be with you, then?" asked *Odious*. "It's not hard for my dad and me to throw our hate bombs—except making them is hard, sometimes."

Love replied, "It's hard to be with me sometimes, because being with me means never insisting on just having your own way. It means being open and generous, fair and unselfish. It means considering the needs of others in addition to just your own."

"Ha!" snorted *Hatred*. "Open and generous, fair and unselfish," he said, mimicking her in his falsetto. "How can you possibly say you're not a lightweight?"

Joy answered quickly, "I said earlier that there's not a blasting agent you can make to overcome *Love*, and it's true. *Love's* strength comes from *Patience*, an ally more powerful than any stick of your dynamite. I promise you that when *Love* packs *Patience* into a cartridge and launches it, she'll 'kill you with kindness,' and then we'll allow *Hope* to spring eternal for generations to come. This is our ultimate and most effective weapon."

"Is it good to be kind?" asked *Odious*, obviously confused.

"Oh, yes, most certainly," responded *Love*. "Especially when you're kind to yourself. I hope you will be kind to yourself as well as to others, *Odious*."

"*Odious*, here's your chance to show *Love* how much you hate her," his father said. "I've just put this grenade together. Throw it at her."

"Dad, that's rude!"

"Of course it's rude!" *Hatred* replied impatiently. "You're supposed to be rude! Only *Love* isn't rude! Don't listen to *Joy* and *Love*! They don't know what they're talking about. *Joy* and *Love*," he continued, addressing them now, "my young *Odious* will be the rudest and most arrogant kid on the block by the time I get through teaching him my poisonous and toxic operating methods. There's nothing you can do about it. Say your prayers now, because he's about to arrange a meeting with your Maker, ha, ha! Go ahead, *Odious*, throw the grenade!"

Religion, who had been silent up until now, said: "Their Maker is here with them now. They walk with Him every day, because He is an eternal part of them. Throwing this grenade won't get the results you want, I promise you that. God is the very essence of *Love*, and it is this *Love* that will eventually destroy you and your evil intent."

Odious, still confused, paused doubtfully. Looking up at *Hatred*, he asked, "Why do I have to do this, Dad? I asked you before, and you didn't really answer me. Why should I throw this grenade, if *Love* will only endure anyway?"

"You don't have the answer, do you, *Hatred*?" *Joy* asked triumphantly. "No matter how much you try, *Love* will always be here, waiting in kindness with *Patience* and her generosity of spirit. I will be here, too, to support them. Your evil bombs and your bullets are not your strength, but your weakness, because our combined forces can obliterate your jealous and angry actions without firing a single shot of physical destruction. As I said before, we'll just 'kill you with kindness.'"

"I don't want to be rude or evil, Dad. I want to be kind," *Odious* announced. He put the grenade down.

"Look what you've done to my kid!" screamed *Hatred*. "You've ruined him! How can I brag to my friends now about what a little monster he is? You know what? I've had it! I'm leaving. This is so embarrassing! My kid, *Odious*, Son of *Hatred*, wants to be kind! The other Joy Robbers will all laugh at me, especially after all the boasting I've done about him. This is too much! You've destroyed me! You've destroyed my life!"

Beginning to weep, *Hatred* hauled himself back up into the hole in the ceiling where he'd come from. Young *Odious* stood there, bewildered, looking from *Joy* to *Love* and then up at the ceiling opening. *Love* approached him and taking his hand, said: "*Odious*, we told you that *Love* endures. Even your father, *Hatred*, must love you somehow. So there's always *Hope* for a happier future, isn't there?"

Odious nodded, his large eyes fixed on *Love's* beauty. But then, slowly he looked down at her hand holding his, and squeezed out of her grasp.

"If I go back up into the ceiling to be with my Daddy, will you be mad at me?" he asked.

"Disappointed, maybe," *Love* answered. "But I'll wait for you to come back for as long as it takes. I promise I'll never terrorize you, steal from you, lie to you, or hurt you. That doesn't mean you can do just whatever you please all the time, especially if it's something naughty. But I will always show *Patience* and be kind to you."

"And if I misbehave? If I secretly take one of Dad's bombs and throw it at someone?"

"Then I will have to discipline you and take away your privileges. Remember that you have a choice, and with every choice you make comes a consequence."

The ceiling started shaking and rattling, more dust falling out of the hole. *Hatred* leaned out and said, "I've come back for *Odious*. Lemme have him."

Joy and *Love* looked at one another. They truly didn't know what to do. The thought of sending *Odious* back to his malicious father was wrenching.

"Well, where is he?" *Hatred* demanded.

"Right here," *Joy* said, turning to where *Odious* had been standing with *Love*. Only *Odious* wasn't there. *Religion* wasn't there, either.

"What have you done with *Odious*?" *Hatred* demanded.

"*Religion* must have taken him somewhere, but we didn't see them go," *Love* responded helpfully. "I think *Religion* took him to an orphanage. We thought you'd abandoned him. I mean, you just left him with us!"

"Well, yes, well, no, well, not really," *Hatred* said, not seeming able to admit what he had done. He felt suddenly overwhelmed at the loss of his only child. How could he continue his legacy with *Odious* gone? Then menacingly, *Hatred* continued, "Looks like I'll have to snatch someone's kid to take his place. Without *Odious* to carry on my mission, I'll lose my stature among the *Joy Robbers*. Thanks for nothing."

"*Hatred*, it sounds like you need some lessons on *Love*," *Joy* commented.

Feeling weakened by the complexity of emotions brought on by his loss, *Hatred* was afraid that he was experiencing *Love* for his child, the very thing he had taught *Odious* not to feel. "No!" he thundered back. "She's already said she'd 'kill me with kindness!' Forget it!"

"Well, then, you can also forget about kidnapping someone else's innocent child, *Hatred*," responded *Joy*, "because I'm going to post my *Joy* SWAT team at your doorstep. You'll never get away from us. You're finished, done with." As *Joy* and *Love* headed towards the exit, *Love* looked back over her shoulder and said, "We'll be back soon." *Joy* added, "Don't bother trying to hide anywhere, because we'll find you, no matter where you go."

Anxiety overwhelmed *Hatred* as his detestable life seemed to flash before his eyes. Feeling suddenly alone, it occurred to him that some of the other *Joy Robbers* ought to be with him and offer their support. He hurried to the telephone and called *Anger*. But *Anger*, upset with *Hatred* over everything and nothing, was screening his calls, and upon seeing *Hatred's* name and number pop up in the caller ID device, he ignored it and laughed.

As *Hatred* hung up the phone in complete disgust, he heard what sounded like the thundering clatter of a giant army in rapid approach. Peering out the window, he saw *Joy's* SWAT team marching in precision, resplendent in their uniforms made of the finest armor. *Joy* and *Love* were leading, followed closely by *Hope*, who was carrying the team's banner, then *Faith, Vision, Patience, Appreciation, Choice, Courage, Peace*, and *The Future*. How smartly they marched, eager to forever vanquish *Hatred* and his evil legacy!

Panicking now, *Hatred* picked up the phone to call the evil twins, *Bitterness* and *Unforgiveness*. Maybe they would prove their loyalty, unlike *Anger*—that miserable traitor! But they were busy stoking the fires at a divorce hearing and told *Hatred* he was on his own.

Beaten, and knowing he could never defeat that powerful army of *Joy Builders* congregated out there, *Hatred* angrily grabbed his walking stick. After attaching to it a small white T-shirt that had once belonged to *Odious*, he began his slow walk to surrender. Still, he paused and mused whether he should try to deploy one last hate bomb before giving up. But *Hatred* was old and getting weak. Shaking his head, annoyed with himself for not being able to overcome *Joy* and his SWAT team, *Hatred* exited the building, where he was instantly surrounded and joyfully taken into custody. He was never heard from again.

7

Joy Meets *Selfishness*

He that falls in love with himself will have no rivals.
— *Benjamin Franklin*

Selfishness was feeling somewhat anxious. She knew it was her day to meet *Joy*, and that she would surprise him because of her dissimilarity to some of the other characters that he had already met. In fact, *Selfishness* knew that *Joy* wanted to replace some of the *Joy Robbers* and coexist with the others, but she was not sure which ones he wanted to replace. However, *Selfishness* was certain that she could convince him of her unique and supreme importance.

When *Joy* arrived, *Selfishness* smiled radiantly and thanked him for his time. After all, he was spending time with her, which is what she expects from everyone. She explained, "I allow my clients to look only at their own needs and wants, and to always put themselves first. It's all about self-absorption, self-centeredness, self-preservation, self-promotion, self-indulgence and self-aggrandizing. You esteem yourself above all others."

She paused, thought to herself for a moment, and then said, "When you do all that I described, why would you need *Joy*?" Laughing aloud, she joked, "Being selfish is what really makes everyone happy. When it's all about them."

"But then what happens to your clients when their loved ones need them or if their community needs them?" *Joy* responded quizzically.

Selfishness answered: "Well, you evaluate what you want to do at all times, and you do only that. Sometimes what you want to do will be what is needed, and sometimes it is not. For instance, I advise my clients not to make themselves team players. I tell them they should operate with a selfish agenda only, and make sure they get what they want at any cost. If my clients work for a company, they simply watch out for their own interests. They may talk about the vision of the organization and all that, but it's pure lip service. If they do it my way, they are looking out only for Number One.

"Sometimes my clients will share their *Selfishness* and extend it to their loved ones. In these cases, my clients look out only for the concerns for those closest to them. They are not interested in serving their communities or their world unless it is something that they believe will ultimately serve the best interests of those closest to them. Their banner cry is "My four and no more." My clients may often say prayers of concern for the people they love, but they would never include people they don't know."

"I don't understand," *Joy* replied. "How would this benefit whatever team they are a part of, or how would it benefit your clients' families?"

Selfishness flashed her radiant smile again and told *Joy* he was truly misunderstanding who she is. "It's not about benefiting others; it's about benefiting you and yours. My clients justify their positions because they believe they and their families should always come first. Don't get me wrong," *Selfishness* continued. "My clients do give; they just give to what gives to them. That's the way we play this game.

"Many of my clients are so self-absorbed, they can turn any topic of conversation into a discussion about themselves or only what's important to themselves. If their self-absorption continually focuses on their negative feelings or opinions, it can lead to melancholy behavior or bad choices. If my clients would choose to listen and respond with interest to others, not only would they feel better, the people around them would, also. This, of course, would take them off my client list, so *Joy*, let's just keep this between me and you."

As *Joy* scribbled his notes, he thought this assignment might be a little more complicated than what he had expected originally. Knowing that he brings much *Joy* to his clients when they give to others, he had not considered their motives for giving. "What else would put you out of business?" he asked *Selfishness*.

"One thing I have learned from some of my past clients is that they must humble themselves, or it will be done for them," she replied. "If my clients took themselves down one notch on the 'importance ladder,' it would change everything. You know, when this happens," *Selfishness* continued, "it rocks my world."

Now even more curious, *Joy* asked *Selfishness* who would go into the number one slot if her clients and their loved ones stepped down a notch. *Selfishness* stopped, looked at *Joy*, then silently pointed upward. After a moment, she said, "Even *Joy Robbers* know that no creature is greater than the Creator."

"So true," replied *Joy*, preparing to wrap up the interview. "Once your clients move God into first place, they automatically become true servants of all mankind."

Joy thanked *Selfishness* for her time and insights; as far as he was concerned, *Selfishness* had solved the crime and identified the resolution for this situation. "I'll work with you, *Selfishness*, but you won't get all my time or attention."

"Well, fine!" she snapped. "Then I won't be sharing anything else with you. You can go now, *Joy*. I'm through with you. Giving anybody anything makes me ill, anyway!"

8

Joy Meets *Betrayal*

When you betray somebody else, you also betray yourself.
— *Isaac Bashevis Singer*

The meeting with *Betrayal* had to be rescheduled many times because, of course, *Betrayal* never keeps a commitment. Finally, the two met. *Betrayal* smiled and shook hands with *Joy*. "I know who you are, but I can't understand why you think you need to talk to me. I'll be honest with you—I'm out to hurt people. Their pain and heartache give me tremendous satisfaction. I know you've met *Selfishness*, but I don't know if she told you that we date and have plans to marry. Our relationship is vital to our operation.

"When I show up for my clients, I sometimes have to appear to be happy and carefree, but that's only to lure them into believing that I'll bring something positive into their lives," *Betrayal* explained candidly. "I usually make friends with my clients and convince them that I am really there for them; but what the poor fools don't realize is that I am a master of deception. You see, I operate with a selfish agenda."

Joy answered: "You really need replacing, but I'm not sure I understand why you even exist. Why do you want your clients to betray their friends, family, or coworkers?"

"Because," Betrayal answered, "what I really want to do is refer them to *Hopelessness* after I'm finished stabbing them in the back, as it were. I know they don't feel the sting of *Betrayal* unless it comes from someone they've loved and trusted."

"Oh," *Joy* gasped in disgust. "That is so cruel! It sounds as if you are admitting that you create *False Love*."

Betrayal nodded. "That's a good way to put it. I usually come out from the depths of *Jealousy* and *Envy*, which is why I don't want to see them replaced. If you do that, you would essentially close down my operation."

"So what would it take to replace you?" *Joy* countered.

"I'll tell you," *Betrayal* answered, "and I hope that the information doesn't get out to the media: when *False Love* meets *Real Love*, it destroys me. I can't keep the deception going forever; it's very tiring, and eventually I run out of energy."

Joy asked *Betrayal* if he had a role model that had helped to shape his operation. "Sure," *Betrayal* answered. "The best example I know of is Judas, the man who betrayed Jesus. Around here, we think of him as a superb role model and one of the *Joy Robber* leaders; however, we are constantly reminded that he hung himself."

Looking steadily at *Betrayal*, *Joy* said: "If you want to know where you are going, simply look at who you are following. Since I just heard you say that you follow Judas, I'd say you're at the end of your rope."

As *Joy* turned to leave, *Betrayal* said: "Maybe you're right. Maybe I'm at the end of my rope. But I'm getting one more shot. *Selfishness* has been getting more clients than I have, and that really makes me envious. To ensure that she doesn't win again, I'm planning to sneak away and have a secret romance with *Vanity*, one of her best friends, a month or so before the wedding. Then I'll arrange it so that *Selfishness* finds out about it in public, in front of all her other friends. I can't wait to see her cry."

"*Betrayal*, you are positive proof that when you combine *Envy* with *Selfish Ambition*, you will generate disorder and evil practices," said *Joy*. "You are definitely on my 'A' list of *Joy Robbers* who will be replaced."

9

Joy Meets *Low Self-esteem*

A person's attitude toward himself has a profound influence on
his attitude toward God, his family, his friends, his future,
and many other significant areas of his life.
— *Bill Gothard*

The first thing *Joy* heard from *Low Self-esteem* was: "Wow. I can't believe you really think I am important enough for an interview."

Joy answered, "Since I don't really understand you, I need to interview you so that I can know how to replace you. The problem here is that you are not a *Circumstance of Life*, you are an *Image of Life*. I am thinking that you belong with a gang of thugs other than the *Joy Robbers*."

"All right," *Low Self-esteem* answered. "If you don't understand, I will tell you the essence of who I am. I look into the mirror alongside my clients and I tell them they simply don't measure up. Call me '*The Diminisher*.' I cause my clients to see an image of something less than what they really are. When they look at themselves, I make them dislike what they see or what they feel. I put blinders on them, too, so they are prevented from appreciating their self-worth.

"Then I make them become obsessed and enamored with impossible, out-of-reach, and unrealistic images created by the media. My clients will never be satisfied with just good health. They are driven to continually follow an image created for them.

"I frustrate people when they look at someone that they believe is more attractive or smarter. And of course, my job is to help them see that most people are better than they are. Once I have them convinced, they stay pretty close to me. In general, my clients keep their feelings suppressed. They hate looking in a mirror, but when they do, I'm the first thing they see."

Somewhat undecided now about whether *Low Self-esteem* might be a *Circumstance of Life* after all, *Joy* asked her if this was something that she creates or that her clients inherit.

"It happens a lot during childhood, when my clients are most vulnerable to the way their sense of themselves and their lives are being shaped. Continual negative words spoken to my clients and constant belittling are essential and will ensure my appearance.

"After my clients grow up," *Low Self-esteem* continued, "I can get them to stay by feeding their minds with real or perceived negative reruns. For instance, if they continually play bad tapes or memories from childhood—or from the world in general—I'll show up and strip them of any *Joy*."

By this time, *Joy* was fed up and indignant. He knew this *Joy Robber* was a sneaky one and had to be replaced like so many others in that smarmy gang of thieves.

"One more question, *Low Self-esteem*," said *Joy*. "What is it that you DON'T want your clients to know?"

Pausing a moment, she answered, "I don't want them to know that their design is not an accident or a mistake. It was actually planned and desired for a purpose. I don't want them to realize that they are fearfully and wonderfully made."

She stopped again, covering her mouth with her hand. "Oh my," *Low-Self-esteem* continued. "I can't believe I've given you such vital information. It could ruin me if my clients found out. "Oh, well," she continued, brightening up. "I'm not worried. Even if some of them knew the information, they wouldn't believe it, and I would still have plenty to do."

"I won't worry if you won't worry," *Joy* answered. "The next time I come around, you'll find your client list shrinking in the best kind of way."

He thanked *Low Self-esteem* for her time and let her know that he would be meeting with *Positive Self-esteem* and together they were going to change her world.

"Before you leave, then, I just want you to know that I'm impressed with you," *Low Self-esteem* replied. This amused *Joy*, and he wondered to himself what it is she actually wanted. *Low Self-esteem* continued, "I think you're a good guy. I just want to warn you about two powerful brothers who constantly try to drag my clients and me under. If you visit them, please be careful. They might arrange for your permanent disappearance."

Thanking her for the interview and the information she had shared, *Joy* told *Low Self-esteem* that he wasn't at all afraid. "I know the big bad brothers' boss; he's the one who arranged the meeting."

10

Joy Meets *Shame* and *Guilt*

Keep your face to the sunshine,
and you cannot see the shadows.
—*Helen Keller*

*J*oy braced himself to meet with the "big bad brothers," *Shame* and *Guilt*. *Low Self-esteem* had referred to them as powerful. *Joy* had decided he would not be intimidated, yet he wanted to see how he could stop their joy-robbing activities. He even thought about giving these two *bandidos* an ultimatum: be out of the lives of his clients by sundown—or else! Although perhaps, *Joy* thought to himself, he was just being influenced by his love for some of the old cowboy movies.

When *Shame* and *Guilt* ambled in, *Joy* mused over their less-than-powerful body language. He thought they acted like they were embarrassed to be seen. *Joy* wondered why *Low Self-esteem* felt they were so commanding. Thanking the brothers for their time first, *Joy* began the conversation by asking them how they acquire their clients. Brother *Shame* responded first, saying that his clients have a problem with forgiveness. Not only are they incapable of forgiving others, they cannot even forgive themselves.

Guilt jumped in, adding: "They can't give themselves permission to make mistakes. Many of our clients are perfectionists, which means they place blame somewhere when things are not perfect. They usually blame themselves, and when this happens, they usually receive a visit from us. Just imagine this lethal combination of perfectionism and blaming, and you can see how we get many of our clients."

Shuddering at the thought, *Joy* continued by asking the brothers what would cause them to lose clients. *Shame* spoke after a brief moment of silence. "If my clients could learn to silence the voice of their worst critic, they could work through their guilt."

"And who is their worst critic?" Joy asked, interested.

This time *Guilt* replied, saying, "They are their own worst critics. Since my clients don't give themselves permission to make mistakes, they don't realize that perfection is not possible."

Shame continued, "This behavior produces an unhealthy self-esteem in our clients, which you already know is a negative, pessimistic, and an overall disapproving view of whatever it is they are doing. What's more, my clients don't understand the awesome power of expressing sincere sorrow for the mistake they have made.

"Acknowledging to yourself and to others that the behavior was a mistake is generally the first step in healing," Shame carried on, "but most of our clients ignore it, thanks to my good buddies, *Pride* and *Ego.* When my clients refuse to take that all-important first step, I know I've done a good job."

"Absolutely," *Guilt* chimed in. "This unhealthy attitude prevents them from realizing that strength can be drawn from weakness. It's a lesson that goes unlearned. Our clients can't seem to understand that they may not be what they should be, but they are not what they used to be, either. Our clients believe that you, *Joy*, are up the road somewhere, out of reach; or that you were with them back in their *Past*, but you somehow slipped away."

"So your clients are dreamers who view their *Future* passively or who don't learn from the *Past*?" *Joy* asked.

"That's the way we see it," said *Shame.*

Joy asked the brothers if other people could put his own clients into the state of *Guilt* and *Shame.*

"Of course they can," *Guilt* answered. He continued, "With two conditions: the first is that these 'other people' would be skilled in manipulative practices; the second is that clients give away their own power."

"Their power? I don't understand. What power is that, *Guilt*?" *Joy* wanted to know.

"The power to 'let no person condemn you,'" *Guilt* replied. "Everyone has issues and comes up short in some area of life, no one being perfect. Therefore, no one has the right to judge or condemn my clients. The problem for my clients is that they lack the strength to reject the hurtful or *False Judgement* of others. Some think they are obligated to accept it."

"In other words," *Shame* continued, clarifying, "our clients give those 'other people' permission to make them feel bad. They accept the *False Judgment* of these 'other people' as true and valid. We're talking about that 'power,' the ability to resist being overcome by *False Judgment*. Our clients have that power, but they don't use it, since in many cases they don't know it's there. If they did know it was there, they would have the strength to resist *False Judgment* and its hurtful condemnation. Our clients would not be turning their power over."

"Of course, condemnation is different from conviction," *Joy* said, interrupting for a moment. "Conviction allows you to see the need for change without beating yourself up. It comes from the power of conscience. It's important that a good and moral conscience is maintained and obeyed."

Picking up where *Shame* left off, *Guilt* added, "Our clients usually arrive with the inability to see beyond their limitations, though, especially those limitations that have been imposed by others who judge them."

Joy stopped the conversation and told them both to look at him in the eye. *Shame* and *Guilt* dropped their heads and replied that they couldn't.

"But why?" *Joy* wanted to know.

"Our job is pretty embarrassing, and we both recognize it," *Guilt* and *Shame* replied.

"Listen to me," Joy admonished the brothers. "What you do can change in just the briefest moment; and the same thing is true for your clients. Whatever it is that you desire, you must first have direct eye contact with it, and then go after it.

"By way of illustration, my job as *Joy* is to get your clients to first look at me and realize that I'm not up the road or in some closet in the past. I'm actually lying within reach, within their very own hearts. My strength will either decrease or increase by the degree to which they desire me."

The brothers suddenly started to feel that they were losing their own strength in the face of *Joy*, and they asked him to leave immediately.

Emboldened by his own clarity and truth, *Joy* said, "I know that you've both led your clients down a one-way street to a blind alley, but I'm going to be there putting up new directional signs for your clients."

Guilt and *Shame* looked at each other. "Weren't you on your way out, *Joy*? What are you talking about, anyway?" they asked.

"Sure, I'm leaving for now," *Joy* countered. "But on my way out, I'm going to put up new signs that say: 'Take a daily left on *Forgiveness*,' 'Take a daily right turn on *Positive Attitude*,' and 'Arrive at the *Healing* and *Joy* intersection.' You two fellows really ought to be ashamed of yourselves for not letting your clients know that I am so close, they can simply reach out and touch me if they wanted to."

Guilt and *Shame* let their heads drop in remorse, both realizing that *Joy's* directional turns certainly would end their job security.

11

Joy Meets *Loneliness*

Loneliness can alienate you from you.
—*Sandra Steen*

"**W**rite an account of my meeting with *Loneliness*," *Joy* noted in his daily planner. "Send the information to the *Joy Builders' Newsletter*."

My Meeting with *Loneliness*: A Personal Account by *Joy*

He wasn't isolated; in fact, he was surrounded by throngs of people milling about, jabbering, chattering, whispering, gossiping, passing their messages around to each other and sometimes to him. In fact, I had difficulty identifying *Loneliness*, as he seemed so much like everyone else. When I finally figured out which one he was, I asked him if we could find a private place for the interview. We left the crowd and he offered me a bottle of water.

When we sat down, I told him I wanted to replace him. When he replied that he thought it would be a good idea because he really would like to leave his post, I was surprised. He told me the job was actually depressing for him. He said he was finding that he was getting more and more clients from all walks of life, and the funny thing was

53

that people mostly thought that he was just busy with single clients. But it turns out that he has been increasingly sneaking into marriages.

Loneliness confessed to me that he was experiencing burnout, and he would welcome replacement. He said that he actually wanted to try doing something positive for his clients, but he wasn't certain that he could, since his only training has been in loneliness.

I was pleased to receive this kind of cooperation, and I told *Loneliness* that it was my guess he was feeling somewhat lonely himself. He responded that he has others with whom he communicates and who send him referrals. His main referral sources are *Broken Relationships* and *Low Self-esteem*; however, the holiday seasons bring him referrals from the whole gang of *Joy Robbers*.

I informed *Loneliness* that it is important for me to understand the reason for the increase of his workload. He explained that *Emptiness* had been collaborating with him, and when the two of them work together, most clients have difficulty finding the solution for eliminating them.

Sometimes their clients try to fill their lives up with more material things. But these material things give nothing back to their owners after the initial thrill of possession wears off. Naturally then, the more of these objects they acquire, the emptier their clients feel and the worse their problem becomes.

I told *Loneliness* how much I appreciated his willingness to give up his post. I assured him that I would do all I could to replace him, but that I would need more information to make a smooth transition.

I started by asking him for the major factors contributing to his (unfortunate) success. *Loneliness* answered that when people don't understand the meaning of *True Fulfillment*, they can't find what they don't recognize. He also said that he once lost a client when she told her friends and family that the only way she could justify being lonely was to believe that having God is not enough—but He *is* enough to meet her every need. Since that amazing revelation, he has not provided services to this client.

Loneliness further explained that you can know who you are, but you must also know "whose you are" to be totally fulfilled. He said that when his clients figure this out, they can be alone and never be lonely.

As *Joy*, I understand this, dear readers, because I know that I am an expression of *True Fulfillment*. I can identify with what *Loneliness* was saying. It makes sense to me because as I interpret what he said, there's that one DIVINE relationship that fulfills you, and then you don't expect anyone else to fulfill you since that has already been accomplished.

[End of newsletter article.]

With his newsletter article completed, *Joy* was ready to move on to the next interview, now that he felt comfortable about how he could replace *Loneliness*.

12

Joy Meets *Great Wealth*

In this world it is not what we take up,
but what we give up, that makes us rich.
—*Henry Ward Beecher*

When *Joy* met *Great Wealth* he envisioned a very short meeting, having assumed that after managing some of the other more difficult interviews, this would be a simple coexistence situation, not a potential replacement meeting. In his mind, he thought: "Who in their right mind could not find *Joy* with *Great Wealth*?"

The mansion, overlooking a luxuriant landscape of native plantings, was a stunning structure, a dazzling architectural wonder, artfully designed in its beauty and splendor. When *Joy* arrived for the interview, the butler ushered him into the stately library, replete with books, leather-bound and gilded, some new, some very old, lovingly thumbed, quietly read.

A single red rose, perfect in its vibrant, shimmering beauty, rested on the gleaming rollaway cart that was brought in moments later. From a steaming hot coffeepot, the butler carefully poured coffee into an enormous cup and saucer made of bone china. Laying an oversized napkin of impossibly white linen monogrammed in red on *Joy's* lap, the butler offered him the finest coffee he had ever tasted in his life. The cream and sugar were dispensed from crystal-cut glass vessels that sparkled in the sunlight brightening the room.

Delighted, intoxicated not just by the rich and smooth taste of the beverage, but by the sumptuous beauty and comfort that surrounded him, *Joy* began to feel at home, especially after comparing this venue to some of the other places he had recently been.

Great Wealth appeared from the French doors that opened out to an elegant garden terrace, with flowers of every shade climbing and tumbling over walls in a glorious riot of color. Well-dressed for the interview and smiling congenially at *Joy*, he welcomed his visitor to his domain. After thanking *Great Wealth* for the gracious reception and commenting on the exquisite surroundings, *Joy* indicated that he was ready to begin the interview.

"I know you want to coexist with me and I have no problems with that," *Great Wealth* said. "I just need to know what you will cost me, because I am a bottom-line kind of guy."

"I don't understand what you mean," *Joy* answered. "What will I cost you? I simply want to coexist with you. I don't want to replace you, and I'm not here for you to buy me."

Great Wealth countered, saying: "You see, I have to look at the cost of everything. I even know how much it costs me to get out of bed in the morning. That's how I've acquired this place you admire so much. I don't mind you joining me, as long as nothing that I own has to go."

"Oh I get it," replied *Joy*. "You only want the joy that comes from possessing great wealth. Is that correct?"

"No need to put it that way, but I can say that if all that I possess were gone, you could not coexist with me. My level of contentment relies on everything that you see here," *Great Wealth* answered matter-of-factly.

Joy said, "Let me ask you this: what are the conditions for which you will allow me to coexist with you?"

"Like I said before," *Great Wealth* responded patiently. "All of my assets, tangible and intangible, must stay intact. I require financial success in every acquisition venture I go on. As long as those conditions are met, then you are welcome to stay. In fact, *Joy*, I would think you would want to just move in and stay here—life in my house is as pampered and pleasurable as a stay at any one of the world's fanciest five-star hotels."

Ignoring that remark, *Joy* asked *Great Wealth* if he had met *Trouble*. "Oh yes, sure I know him. But I've paid him off in every single category," *Great Wealth* answered. "While I realize there are some areas in which I may not be protected, for the most part my treasures provide my clients with everything that they need."

"Look, *Great Wealth*," *Joy* responded. "Of course, I am certainly willing to coexist with you, but you should know that I want to be here unconditionally."

Great Wealth shook his head slowly, saying: "I'll be honest with you. My clients have all bought their joy. My goal is to keep them so attached to their personal score cards, that they continuously desire even more wealth. I teach them that there is no such thing as 'enough.'

"Some of my clients have been quoted as saying that even when they had cars, homes and lots of everything, they still weren't happy on the inside, believe it or not. In some of my worst cases, clients have even turned to drugs or alcohol, thinking that somehow they could experience inner joy, at least while the substances were buzzing and burning in their brains. As their personal representative, I just want them to stay attached to their wealth, because I like it, too. I don't care where their joy comes from. Just as long as we all have piles of money.

"*Joy*," *Great Wealth* concluded, clapping and then rubbing his hands together, "if you can work with that, then we have a deal."

"You don't care where their happiness comes from? I certainly care, so as far as I'm concerned, you and I have no deal at all. Anybody can experience 'gladness of heart' when life is dealing you all the right cards and you can live in a place like this with hardly a worry to bother with," *Joy* continued. "However, I am far more authentic than just existing as a word when things are truly going well, or when clients deliberately alter and abuse their minds in their quest to find me."

Great Wealth said nothing.

Joy continued, "I am interested in clients who want to experience what I bring, no matter what the stakes are. I know you have the kind of wealth that can buy you almost anything. However, 'almost' is the operative word here. Just tell your clients to call me when they are interested in something that money can't buy."

13

Joy Meets *Anger*

A gentle answer turns away wrath,
but a harsh word stirs up anger.
—Proverbs 15:1

A fool gives vent to his anger,
but a wise man keeps himself under control.
—Proverbs 29:11

It felt so strange—as if *Joy* were looking at whom he could possibly be if he were not actually *Joy* himself. "This is so weird," he thought, "as if I were looking at my own polar opposite in some sort of reverse mirror."

Joy extended his hand for the perfunctory handshake of introduction, but *Anger* just stared at him coldly and kept his arms folded across his chest. "This will go well," *Joy* laughed to himself as he pulled out his notebook.

He started by asking *Anger* how it is that he occupies so much space in the hearts and minds of clients. *Anger* replied that he receives a generous amount of help from the rest of the *Joy Robbers*, so he couldn't take all the credit. All had in some way helped him expand his territory, but it angered him that he was sometimes overwhelmed with clients.

"So what is it that brings you out in your clients?" *Joy* asked, careful not to irritate *Anger* any further.

Anger replied, "I come from my client's emotions, a place that many don't try to manage or control. My clients are often mad at the world because of some unresolved issue they have not dealt with. Many remain angry because they refuse to release *Bitterness.*"

"You know, *Anger,*" *Joy* said pensively, "you can serve a good purpose. I've seen some people who have used you to change a bad situation."

"True, but to keep you out," *Anger* replied, "I need to distort reality and cause my clients to take out their rage on people, institutions, or principles. This gives me a double edge, because my negative but powerful emotion infects those giving it as well as those receiving it. My job is to perpetuate tension rather than resolution. Resentment and anger can truly destroy lives. Whether my clients can identify their anger, or whether they no longer know the source of their anger, it can lead to great unhappiness.

"If I can keep my clients in a constant state of fury, some will find ways to medicate themselves, often leading them to drug or alcohol abuse. Oh, the sheer drama and intensity of it all! That's what feeds their anger.

"It's a veritable feast of venom, a bacchanalian banquet of trembling and shrieking wrath that I serve up to my clients with the vilest of passions. Of course, I understand I have various functions, but at the end of the day, I'm just there to make them miserable and unhappy."

Joy finished writing his notes and looked up at this most unattractive *Joy Robber.* "So, what do you think it will take for me to replace you?" he asked *Anger.*

The rage came in its fullest manifestation. *Anger* raised his voice, and pounding his fist down on the interview table, he yelled, "You don't need to replace me, because without me, *Anger,* what reason would my clients have to be miserable? I represent a choice, and I must continue to fulfill the choice my clients have to be angry with whomever they choose."

Standing up now and gesturing wildly, *Anger* continued his loud objection: "Anyway, *Joy*, if you really want to replace me, you'll need to talk to *Hatred*, and to *Bitterness* and *Unforgiveness*, because I get a lot of their clients." This time, *Anger* pounded his fist into the wall.

Joy sat there patiently listening to all *Anger* had to say. Then he slowly stood up. Walking directly up to *Anger* and speaking to him at a distance of less than an inch, *Joy* replied, "*Anger*, I'm not afraid of you. You can punch the walls or kick the table to show what a big, intimidating *Joy Robber* you are, but you won't scare me away.

"I hope you're done with your angry little performance, because you need to calm down. You know, if you keep this kind of emotional energy going, you will shorten the life of your clients. I've read independent research studies that report on the effects of your kind of emotion. When your clients combine their anger with resentment, they double their risk of a heart attack. *Anger*, you can become a deadly emotion for them, indeed."

Joy stepped away from *Anger* and sat down again. He continued, in a softened tone. "*Anger*, you really do have a place in your clients' lives, as long as they don't go out of control and do something crazy because of their anger. You are a natural occurrence; an instinctive displeasure your clients feel when real or perceived mistreatment and even injury takes place. I understand that even in a relationship with someone you love and care about, you can experience temporary anger towards him or her."

Joy paused for a moment to let *Anger* absorb this information, and then continued: "The key action for your clients is to not let the sun go down on their anger. If they can commit to this, if they can understand what it means for themselves and whoever is the object of their anger, your clients can prevent their emotions from destroying their relationships—and themselves. If your clients would begin to identify the object and the cause of their anger, they would often find that the result of their resentment is causing costly negative effects on them and the people they care about. The important question for your clients is this: Is being constantly angry worth the losses?"

Seeming to calm himself as he listened to *Joy*, *Anger* became impressed with *Joy's* knowledge of human emotion. "I personally don't know the answer to that," he answered. "Only my clients would know. Not to change the subject, but one of my busiest times is during rush hour the world over," he told *Joy*.

"Actually, I've heard that same thing about rush hour from my joyous clients, too, who call on me when your angry clients are making certain impolite hand gestures in traffic," *Joy* responded. "They call me because they don't want to lose their connection with me when your clients are teetering on road rage, insulting them, and engaging in episodes of generally bad behavior.

"Listen, *Anger*, I'll go ahead and do more work with your clients," *Joy* continued. "Just let me remind you that although *Hatred, Bitterness*, and *Unforgiveness* are sending you clients, the responsibility is yours to foster their emotional growth. You should also do more to get your clients to use their anger in a positive way."

Anger agreed, though hesitantly. Then, in a moment of honesty, he admitted that his blood pressure was elevated and the stress of his position was causing him headaches.

"*Anger,* I think you have discovered a very good reason for my presence in your life," *Joy* said quietly.

14

Joy Meets *Bitterness* and *Unforgiveness*

When you forgive, you in no way change the past—
but you sure do change the future.
— *Bernard Meltzer*

Deeply affected by his meeting with *Anger*, *Joy* decided immediately that he must get to the terrible twins, *Bitterness* and *Unforgiveness*, to arrange for replacement. *Bitterness* and *Unforgiveness* met him at the door, and immediately began bragging about their incredible memory.

They told *Joy* they could remember every bad thing anyone has ever done to their clients. Their duties include helping their clients to not just remember, but constantly replay the offending incidents. Clients often record the wrong in their journals so that *Bitterness* and *Unforgiveness* can constantly function. This memory drill results in a constant bombardment of negative thoughts.

Amazed at how well they were working together, *Joy* asked if one could function without the other. They looked at one another and then smiled. "We're joined at the hip," they said in unison. "We always function together."

"And how is it that you have been so successful at maintaining such a large client base?" *Joy* asked.

"Pain has an incredible way of allowing my clients to justify the act of not forgiving," *Unforgiveness* began. "Some believe that as long as the pain is there, unforgiveness should remain. Of course, I encourage this thinking. Once the pain is gone, some of my clients believe I should remain until someone else is given the same pain that they received. My clients believe that everyone should be properly repaid for their wrong; of course, they believe that God and man should keep no account of their wrongs."

Joy nodded thoughtfully, reflecting on these words. Some of what the twins were saying was making more sense to him than what he wanted to admit. Finding an opening to replace these powerful twins had just become vitally important to his own existence.

"'You reap what you sow.' 'What goes around comes around.' Have either of you heard those two sayings before?" *Joy* asked them.

"Ah, yes," *Bitterness* replied. "The concepts of reward and punishment, accountability and responsibility. Of course we've heard those before! But we don't exist because of what someone did to our clients; we exist in how our clients choose to respond. It's our trade secret."

Unforgiveness said, "We would be out of work if our worldwide clients find out that they can forgive as a choice and be free of the painful memory. Even a half-hearted decision to merely think about the possibility of forgiveness starts to lessen the hurt and anger."

Joy perked up, because the twins were unwittingly giving him the answer he was looking for. He asked the twins how most of their clients would describe doing business with them.

The twins looked at each other, puzzled, then conferred in quick whispers. "Well," *Bitterness* ventured, "I guess the best image we can come up with is that of a jail cell. When we work together, our clients are often locked up emotionally and can't experience true joy."

"I add special effects," *Unforgiveness* boasted. "When our clients put themselves into the state of unforgiveness, I harden their hearts and prevent them from experiencing warm thoughts. I like it bitter and mean like that.

"Our clients somehow feel they have taken the appropriate action against their violators by harboring bitterness and unforgiveness, but in fact it is our clients themselves who are the ones most affected. We often disguise ourselves in justification, which makes them think that they are deserving of us, somehow."

Joy asked, "What would help to break this harmful cycle for your clients?"

Unforgiveness replied, "If our clients truly understood that forgiveness does not have to condone or approve harmful acts, they would enter the sphere of healing. Forgiveness is for the doer, not the doing. The real tragedy for our clients is that they cannot receive forgiveness from God if they don't learn to extend forgiveness to others. Most of the time, our clients just ignore this important fact. To help our clients ignore this truth, we do everything we can to distort it."

"Thank you for your time," Joy said, indicating the close of the interview. "Just to set the record straight, I don't want to coexist with you. You need to know that I really want to replace you."

"You truly have your work cut out for you," Bitterness said laughing, "because you would be surprised at the number of clients we have worldwide."

"However, we hope you meet with at least some success," Unforgiveness added, "because we could really use a vacation."

15

Joy Meets *Worry*

Worry does not help anything, but it hurts everything.
—*General George S. Patton*

When *Joy* met *Worry*, she was frantically pacing back and forth, a frenzied look on her face. She had not noticed that *Joy* had arrived; up and down she paced, biting her fingernails. *Joy* stood there for a moment, considering the best way to get her attention. Finally *Joy* shouted, "Hey, *Worry*, did you remember we had an appointment today?"

Startled, *Worry* jumped, gasped, and then apologized to *Joy* for not realizing that he had been standing there.

Joy started the conversation by asking *Worry* why she was pacing so much. *Worry* answered, "It's part of my job description. I keep my clients in an anxious frenzy so they don't have time to engage in rational thinking. I'm the 'what-if' queen.

"I don't want my clients to act calmly or to meditate, because they may think of a way to eliminate me," *Worry* continued. "To remain with my clients, I have to cloud their minds with false fears and ridiculous assumptions."

"Is that how you get your clients?" *Joy* asked.

"For the most part," responded *Worry*. "*Fear* sends me most of my referrals. Since he is my neighbor, it's easy for us to get together. I am grateful to *Fear* and frankly would not be as successful without his help.

"Because *Fear* and other *Joy Robbers* help me so much, I have to say that it upsets me terribly when people blame me and me alone for things like premature aging in my clients. Also, world-renowned scientists are giving me and me alone credit for certain grave diseases. This smear campaign is all so insensitive!"

Joy was writing quickly. *Worry* was giving him excellent information, and he didn't want to miss any of it. "I'm not certain if I should coexist with you or just go ahead and replace you," he said. "What do you think I should do, *Worry?*" *Joy* asked.

Worry paused and then began pacing franticly again. Concerned that she would give him the wrong answer, she suddenly went into a severe panic attack, right in front of *Joy*. Grabbing her by the arms, *Joy* told *Worry* to settle down. He would relieve her of anxiety, he said, because she had just given him the answer.

Quieting down, *Worry* began fretfully rocking from side to side. She hardly heard what *Joy* was saying, so overwhelmed and distracted had she become.

"You have a great deal on your mind, *Worry*," *Joy* said. "I understand perfectly that you are simply doing your job effectively, but I want to ask you one last question before I leave.

"*Worry*," he began, "I definitely know that I want to replace you. But tell me what could most of your clients do that would remove them from your client list?"

She stopped pacing and looked at *Joy*. "What I'm about to tell you is hard for me to say, but I will try." *Worry* began crying. "My biggest fear is that my clients will meet *Peace* and they will no longer need me. *Joy*, surely you won't introduce them to the kind of peace that surpasses their understanding. Don't you understand that if you do, I will be an unemployment statistic?"

"I understand your worries, but sometimes you can create monsters with your thoughts, and that's completely unnecessary. I want to thank you for your honesty," *Joy* continued, "and if it's any consolation, your replacement will be gradual, so try not to fret so much. I'll be in touch."

16

Joy Meets *Fear*

The remarkable thing about fearing God is that
when you fear God, you fear nothing else;
whereas if you do not fear God, you fear everything else.
—*Oswald Chambers*

*J*oy was a little tired after his meeting with *Worry*, having been disturbed by her fretful episodes. But since *Fear* lived right next door, Joy decided to conduct his next interview with him, since he was in the neighborhood.

Joy knocked on the door. Silence. He knocked again. More silence. Then *Joy* realized that he was being peered at from the peephole in the door. "I'm *Joy*," he called out so that *Fear* could hear him. I just came from visiting with your neighbor *Worry*, and am hoping that I can ask for a little time to meet with you, too."

Silence. Then a clicking sound was heard, then another, another and another, followed by some scraping noises and a clunk, and then finally, a thump. *Fear* had so many locks on the door that it took a moment before he could actually open it. *Fear* peered out at *Joy* with suspicion.

"Yeah," he said. "*Worry* just called and said she met you, but I don't trust anyone. Before I let you in, I would like to see some form of identification so I can be certain that you are whom you say you are. After all, there are a lot of scam artists running around, and the rest of us honest *Joy Robbers* are all just trying to make a living."

It was a good thing that *Joy* had his "Gladness of Heart" ID with him; otherwise, *Fear* might have kept him out on the porch. *Joy* thanked *Fear* for finally letting him in and asked if *Fear's* client list had been increasing.

Fear laughed. "Are you kidding? I have so many clients I can barely keep up with the demand!" he exclaimed.

Joy asked *Fear* what he thought was contributing to his increase in business.

"I have to give a lot of credit to my friends in the media, because they help feed my clients," *Fear* replied.

Not understanding what this meant, *Joy* asked *Fear* to clarify his answer.

"Well, *Joy*, it's like this: my clients want to be well informed. It's the abundance of information that at times contributes to their fears. I teach my clients to take the information and exaggerate it with great intensity. I make false evidence appear real. So whether they check on the latest security code colors for a terrorist attack or they find the latest information about the food they are eating, I want them to exaggerate this information. Rather than become informed by it, I want them to become fearful of it. You see, I am often a connection to what my clients fear the most. If they aren't careful, I'll bring to them the very thing that they are afraid of.

"You should know, *Joy*, that fears often have rank and can even cancel each other out. Let me give you an example: a client who is in constant fear about losing his job would not be thinking about that particular fear if he suddenly found himself in a life-threatening situation. Instead, he would now fear dying a sudden and possibly painful death. Here's the lesson. When my clients do their highest thinking about their biggest and most significant fear, and then follow up by eliminating that fear, they will also cancel most of the other little fears that are lurking around their minds."

Joy decided to ask *Fear* a direct question: "What could put you out of business, then?"

Fear's reply was delivered somewhat arrogantly. "I have no fear of being replaced," he said with a haughty air, "because to eliminate me, 'The Big Three' would have to perform their work in perfect unison."

Joy became curious. "'The Big Three?' Who are they?"

With impatience, *Fear* said: "You should know: Love, Power, and a Sound Mind. Do you know how hard it is to maintain all three functioning properly at the same time? To further complicate things, I produce a lack of trust in my clients. In this state of mind, they can't truly love anyone, nor benefit from being of sound mind. How can they, if they can't trust anything or anyone?

"I feel very secure in my position, but if you really think you can replace me, go ahead give it your best shot. You should be aware that I have another division within my organization that provides a normal function for my clients. It's pretty boring, but that job is to create what I call 'normal fear.' It's what keeps my clients from doing stupid things, like taking unnecessary risks. It's mostly our training division. They stay busy teaching children not to talk to strangers, or not to touch a hot stove—basically things like that."

Joy replied, "I have to thank you for that, *Fear*. In some instances, you are actually a gift that warns your clients when they are in danger. But at the same time, you are compassionate enough to protect your clients even while providing them with irrational fears and a distortion of life. "I don't want to replace your entire organization, but I would seek to replace you for clients who desperately need me. By the way, *Fear*, I must tell you that there is one fear that your clients should allow to work for them."

Fear looked very scared when he heard this. "What fear did I not mention?" he asked nervously.

"The fear of God," replied *Joy*. "This fear is known as the beginning of wisdom."

"Hmm, my clients would be prudent, then, if they would live with reverence for God, obey His laws, and thereby grow in the wisdom you speak of," commented *Fear*, who by now appeared to be a little less nervous. "Right?" he asked *Joy*. Now *Fear* seemed nervous again.

"Yes, you are correct," *Joy* answered, realizing this Joy Robber definitely had a split personality. They shook hands and exchanged business cards. *Joy* let *Fear* know they would be staying in touch, and that there was need to be afraid of him.

"Oh, I almost forgot! I have something for you, *Fear*," Joy said, smiling as he reached into his briefcase. "It's an important little token of my disapproval of your work. In fact, this gift from me will serve as an important reminder of your pending future."

Fear seemed puzzled, as he could not imagine receiving a gift from *Joy*, especially one in disapproval of his work. *Joy* handed him a box that was not wrapped but was carefully taped closed.

Fear hesitated, looking at the box with suspicion.

"Go ahead, open it!" *Joy* urged, still smiling, and pressing the box into *Fear's* hands.

As *Fear* began removing the tape, his facial expressions went from puzzlement to curiosity, and then finally to exasperation. The gift he pulled out appeared to be an article of clothing, a T-shirt with a quotation of some sort printed on the front.

Fear squinted disapprovingly at the print on the shirt and with loud exasperation said, "I can't believe that you expect me to wear a 'NO FEAR' T-shirt!"

Joy laughed. "I just wanted to introduce you to what your clients will be wearing this season." As *Joy* began to leave, he told *Fear* he could keep the T-shirt and advertise his future to himself and his clients.

17

Joy Meets *Humor*

Laughter is the shortest distance between two people.
— *Victor Borge*

*J*oy was up for a change of pace. He was so glad his next meeting was with one of his favorite *Joy Builders*, *Humor*! *Humor* was such fun, always full of laughter. *Joy* looked forward to this interview. When he arrived, *Humor* was his usual jovial self and immediately invited *Joy* in. The house seemed to be heaving and rolling with laughter so contagious that *Joy* himself began laughing too, for no apparent reason.

"*Hey, Joy!*" *Humor* said, guffawing. "What do you get when you mix laughter and a merry heart together?"

"I'm not sure," *Joy* replied. "What do you get?"

"You get merry medicine!" *Humor* answered, roaring with laughter and slapping his knee. "You see, I'm good for what ails my clients. My job is to get them to lighten up and enjoy their lives—to find laughter everywhere.

"You know, it's been medically proven that laughter produces endorphins that aid the healing process," Humor continued. "I've heard that for some serious diseases, hospitals will actually hire comedians to help promote healing among their clients through laughter. *Joy*, don't you think this is all just the best and most wonderful evidence of the good that we bring our clients?"

Ah, it was so much fun being around *Humor*! *Joy* smiled in agreement, grinning so hard that his face ached. He could hardly help it.

"So *Joy*," *Humor* continued. "Show me what you've got there — what are you working on these days?"

"I've begun a quest to bring more joy to more clients," *Joy* replied. "At the same time, my project calls for eliminating the *Joy Robbers*."

"Interesting!" replied *Humor*. "See, that's what I want to do. In fact, I'm developing a super-humor virus for all my clients. I'm making it so contagious, that more and more people will catch it every day.

"Actually, I've already made it almost universal for female clients. Most of them are demanding a humor test from males they choose to date and marry. 'Infectious humor' and 'infectious laughter' are what the ladies are looking for these days. The test for my infectious super-humor virus has certainly become a popular dating pastime!"

Chortling, *Humor* continued, "Hey *Joy*, listen to this one! The teacher asks the little boy how many husbands a woman can have at any given time. And the little boy, who had just recently attended a wedding, says, "I know, I know! Sixteen husbands!" The teacher gets all perplexed and asks the little boy where he came up with that number. And so the little boy says to her, '4 Better, 4 Worse, 4 Richer, and 4 Poorer. That equals 16!'"

Joy laughed out loud.

"That's what I want," *Humor* said happily. "Lots of laughter! Then I know that I'm doing my job."

"You'll get lots of laughs with that one! Listen, *Humor*, since we're automatic partners," *Joy* continued, "I'd like to see how we could increase both our workloads and at the same time, improve our performance measurements for humor and joyfulness."

Humor, knowing that there is a time for laughter and a time for seriousness, told *Joy* that his clients find him in positive attitudes and diminished egos. *Joy* started laughing politely. Then he realized *Humor* wasn't making a joke, but was giving him important information. *Joy* took out his notepad and began writing what he had just heard.

"You don't have to wait for someone to join in the fun," *Humor* continued. "My clients can have a party by themselves and laugh, even if they're laughing alone. This means they've acquired the skill of not taking themselves too seriously. They've learned to laugh at themselves when appropriate, which goes back to my earlier point of diminished egos.

"On the other hand," *Humor* added, "I have worked with some clients who know only how to hide their pain with laughter. That is not true humor. I'm not a masquerade character. I work with my clients to help them find me with a light and sincere heart."

Humor continued, "It's out of the abundance of the heart that the mouth will speak. So, I don't just get my clients to crack jokes. I work on getting humor into their hearts, and their mouths will speak from there."

"How do you teach your clients to find you?" *Joy* asked.

Humor responded, "I simply instruct them to look for me everywhere. It's so wonderful to watch my clients finding humor even during their most challenging times. When they find me, I often bring them comfort and serenity."

"Can this make your clients somewhat cynical, for example, if they think it's humorous to laugh at everything and everyone?" *Joy* asked.

"When my clients combine sensitivity, good judgment, and good character with humor, they will always be in good taste," *Humor* answered.

"They will choose to laugh *with* others and never laugh *at* others. It is important to understand that the funniest comments made about you can still be painful. Humor should not be used as a weapon to hurt someone. That's why the motive in your heart is very important in humor. The bottom line for me, *Joy*, is that everyone finds time for appropriate humor."

Joy nodded. "Makes sense," he said, snapping his notebook closed. "Well, *Humor*, it's so hard to leave this atmosphere of laughter and fun, but I must move on for my next interview and 'feel the love,' as some tend to say."

Humor began laughing loudly again. "Your next interview? *Joy*, are you trying to take over Oprah's job?" he asked playfully.

Joy smiled. "Oprah has done a good job of helping me to eliminate some of the *Joy Robbers*, for which my clients and I are most thankful.

"So long, *Humor*. Let's keep the laughter going for all of our clients, and make sure they don't take themselves too seriously. And good luck with your super-humor virus! May you spread it all over and infect the world, joyfully!"

18

Joy Meets *False Joy*

No man truly has joy unless he lives in love.
—*St. Thomas Aquinas*

Now that *Joy* had interviewed several *Joy Robbers* and one of the *Joy Builders*, he decided that this was a good time to review his notes. As he read them and evaluated everything that had transpired, an uneasy feeling came over him. Joy became suspicious that he was being impersonated. Something wasn't right. Something about the interviews with *Jealousy, Low Self-esteem,* and *Great Wealth* was amiss.

He couldn't shake the feeling. He knew he needed to get on top of the problem immediately. *Joy* made a few phone calls, asking if anyone knew of someone using false identification, purporting to be himself, *Joy,* but who was really not.

After talking to *Low Self-esteem,* he got his best clue. She said that she had met with someone claiming to be *Joy's* cousin and business partner. The 'cousin' told her that they could work together, and all she would need to do is help her clients develop a sense of false humility or one of counterfeit joy. "He told me his name was *False Joy,*" *Low Self-esteem* said, and she told *Joy* where to find him.

Irritated, *Joy* hung up. Snatching up his keys and flying out the door, he jumped into his late-model Joy Rider and headed over to the address he now had for *False Joy*. Business partner, indeed! And cousin? This guy had a lot of nerve, trying to disparage *Joy's* good name and that of his real family. *Joy* couldn't wait to confront him.

As *Joy* roared up to the address at 1234 Counterfeit Lane, he realized that the street, the homes, the entire surroundings, were almost identical to his. Amazing! There was even what appeared to be another Joy Rider stationed under the portico. It had smiley-face bumper stickers plastered all over it. Upon closer inspection, however, *Joy* realized that this was nothing but a knock-off of his own unique and original Joy Rider. In fact, everything about the place appeared to be a copy, a poor substitute for all that *Joy* had at home and at work that was original and genuine. This *Joy Robber's* entire existence appeared to be counterfeit.

Joy knocked loudly on *False Joy's* door, ready for a confrontation. He was ready to do whatever he could to stop this case of identity theft.

False Joy, wearing an outfit identical to the one that *Joy* was wearing, answered the door and cordially invited *Joy* in. *False Joy* started the conversation by telling *Joy* that he had expected this meeting sooner, and was glad to finally meet him in person. *False Joy* had studied *Joy* for many years.

"I am aware of what you've been doing," *Joy* responded, "and it has to stop. I have been working very hard to create a better life for my clients, and it's unfair for someone with no credentials to run around trying to impersonate me."

False Joy replied, "Well, I tell you, I'm just creating an option for some clients who can't take the pressure that you bring."

"*Pressure?* You've got to be kidding!" *Joy's* response was passionate. "I don't bring pressure, I bring *relief*. Don't insult me with your false accusations of bringing pressure, when what I really do is bring gladness of heart to my clients."

Then he calmed down, realizing that he still needed to understand his enemy in order to destroy him. *Joy* took out his notepad and asked *False Joy* to explain his function.

"I represent deception," *False Joy* answered. "I am the counterfeit option for those who don't want to pay the price for the real thing, you know, like a copy of a designer handbag."

"Uh-huh." *Joy* maintained his calm demeanor. "And what do you consider the price of joy?" he queried.

False Joy said, "Your clients have to experience you when things are both good or bad. I, however, give them an option of experiencing me only when things are good or only appear to be good."

"So what do you do for your clients when things are bad?" *Joy* asked.

"Well, they don't experience me. They experience one of the *Joy Robbers*, and I just step aside," was the reply.

"So whom are you partnering with?" *Joy* wanted to know.

"I'm working with *Great Wealth* right now," *False Joy* replied, "and I have a whole list of clients who will experience me when they get their awards or when they get approved for their next project. I'm only there temporarily, but at least they have an option to focus more on me or some of my joy-robbing partners."

More irritated than before, *Joy* made it clear that gladness of heart never has to go away in good times or bad, and that he intended to do all in his power to bring an end to the fraudulent practices of *False Joy*.

"Your clients will come to recognize my authenticity when they meet with *Trouble*," *Joy* told *False Joy*. "*Trouble* visits all of our clients, and only real joy will work when he shows up."

Joy continued, "Anyway, *False Joy*, no one truly desires the counterfeit; they just settle for it when they feel they cannot afford the real thing. I'm pretty sure *Rejection* will be arriving at your place soon. Here's my card, if you need my help!"

Joy Meets *Trouble*

The ultimate measure of a man is not where he stands
In moments of comfort and convenience, but where he stands
during challenge and controversy.
— *Martin Luther King*

Of course, *Joy* knew about *Trouble* and actually had respect for him, because he knew that *Trouble* helps his clients to mature and become stronger. He also knew that his clients do not like it when *Trouble* arrives, because most of the time, it is not a pleasant experience. So *Joy* was prepared to work a partnering deal with *Trouble*, but he knew that to work effectively with him, he would have to understand his operation.

Joy met *Trouble* for lunch, but *Trouble* was running late because his car would not start, and then he had a flat tire and got caught in traffic. *Joy* waited patiently for *Trouble* to arrive, deciding to have a light snack in the meantime. To his dismay, when his snack arrived, it wasn't what he had ordered. He laughed to himself. Now *Joy* knew he was on *Trouble's* schedule, and this could be a difficult meeting. *Joy* smiled kindly at the embarrassed waiter and reordered his snack.

In walked *Trouble*. No wonder people always say, "Here comes trouble," *Joy* thought to himself when he spotted the poor unfortunate *Joy Robber*. *Joy* noticed how everyone in the restaurant shunned him, rolling their eyes and looking away when *Trouble* entered, tripping in the doorway. No one offered to help him up.

After gracefully getting back up on his feet and collecting the papers that had fallen out of his briefcase, *Trouble* strode confidently over to the table where *Joy* was waiting for him. "Please, *Trouble*, don't trip again and land on my snack," *Joy* prayed silently to himself.

Trouble had a firm handshake, and *Joy* noticed how powerful his presence was. *Joy* took out his notes and started the interview by congratulating *Trouble* on the way he creates strength in his clients. He also told *Trouble* that he believed a partnership between the two of them would be an excellent proposition, because *Trouble* would be creating strength in his clients while he, *Joy*, would bless them with gladness of heart. *Trouble* could benefit from this partnership, *Joy* explained, because *Trouble* is defeated eventually by the good cheer in their clients.

Trouble nodded. "I understand what you're trying to do, *Joy*," he said. "I'd like to help you. But it's really hard to get my clients to even smile when I show up. Look how all these people behaved when I tripped in the doorway," he continued glumly, resting his chin on his hand, his elbow landing in a dish of hot sauce for *Joy's* snack.

As *Joy* watched *Trouble*, he felt compassion for him. *Joy* asked him what he thought his clients needed to know that would help them in this proposed partnership. *Trouble* said, "Well, *Joy*, it's a hard concept but my clients have to realize that 'in their life they will have trouble.' But they must understand that I do not have the strength to destroy the '*Peace of God*' or a *Positive Attitude* if they have it. I find that a client who maintains good cheer and a connection to God defeats me like a strong conqueror.

"Don't get me wrong! I can get creative and bring a number of difficult situations to my clients, but I don't have the power to take their *Peace* or their positive perspective. They, however, have the power to give it up."

Joy was delighted and intrigued with *Trouble's* wisdom. "Where do you suggest to your clients that they can find *Peace* and *Positive Attitude*?" *Joy* wanted to know.

Trouble looked up briefly at *Joy* and said: "You know, if my clients would just understand that I don't come to stay, they can weather the storm. They will find that after the darkest of nights the sun will still come up the next day. Sometimes clients believe I am there because they did something wrong. They must remember I serve both the righteous and the unrighteous. Ironically, the righteous tend to see a lot of me, but they conquer me with great vigor every single time." *Trouble* paused for a moment, taking off his glasses to clean them. They broke.

"Rats! Oh, well, I just happen to have a spare set of glasses right here in my briefcase," he said, indicating the briefcase he had placed on the table when he had arrived. *Trouble* leaned over to get the spare glasses, dragging his tie in the salsa dish as he did so.

"I've been around the block," he continued, hardly seeming to notice his social gaffe. "I've been around since ancient times. If my clients looked through history, they would find two truths: the first is that if they hold on to what is good, I won't be forever in their lives. The second truth is that if they learn from past 'lessons' I have taught them, I don't need to come around again for another cycle of the same tribulations. My clients must combine obedience with good observation, which will prevent continually repeating my performances."

"Wow, *Trouble*!" *Joy* said. "I think your observations are both remarkable and profound! I believe that ours will be a splendid partnership! I think we should order our lunch now, don't you? Where's our waiter?"

As he looked around for the waiter, *Joy* thought about how much *Trouble's* clients are in need of his services, and how beneficial their partnership would be for the clients. *Joy* was excited about this new prospect. He spotted the waiter. "We're ready to order now," he called out.

"Sorry, sir, kitchen's closed," answered the waiter.

20

Joy Meets *Insecurity*

Sometimes your greatest potential and your
lack of confidence have to coexist.
—*Sandra Steen*

*J*oy had scheduled a meeting with *Insecurity* at the recommendation
of *Jealousy* and *Low Self-esteem*. He didn't know much about
Insecurity, but he had heard that she could be a real joy-buster. Now
he was up to the adventure of finding out if he could partner with her,
or if perhaps he needed to replace her.

Insecurity arrived dressed in the finest apparel *Joy* had ever seen.
Swathed in pearled silk accented with exquisite lace, she was matched
from head to toe in a stunning ensemble of fashion and good taste.
Her hat, belt, gloves, and shoes were of finely stitched suede, her
earrings, necklace, and other jewelry simple but classic.

Joy began by introducing himself and letting her know that he
was there to see how he could assist her clients. *Joy* asked *Insecurity*
to explain her function and its benefits to her clients.

Removing her gloves and draping them softly over her handbag,
she replied quickly. "Well, I work a great deal with *Low Self-esteem*,
and my clients are always feeling threatened. They become so upset
and disoriented from the perceived danger, they will often misjudge a
situation. My clients tend to feel everyone is out to get them. Even if

they have been blessed with talent or good looks, they feel they are at risk. They tend to be easily offended. It's so bad that they often go around hunting for every opportunity to feel insulted, even if there is no intention by others to insult them.

"My function is to keep them from seeing their true potential and to ensure that they don't get along easily with others. Of course, I do need help occasionally from *Jealousy* and *Low Self-esteem* to keep this scheme going, but sometimes it seems to work well without them, too. My clientele is large and growing."

"Really!" *Joy* responded. "I just can't imagine the insecurity that you project for your clients, because you are the picture of confidence! Your outfit is gorgeous. Why, you look like you just stepped off a fashion runway in Paris! I can't keep my eyes off you!"

"Do you see what I mean?" *Insecurity* answered. "Why are you always watching me? Are you looking for me to slip up in any way? Can't wait to catch me making a mistake? Actually, my outfit is just a cover for the lack of confidence I feel. It cost me a fortune, believe me, and I had to borrow money to buy it. But it fools everyone— even fooled you!"

"Fascinating," commented *Joy*. "So, *Insecurity*, what would put you out of business?"

"Well, that's an interesting question and I can answer that in just a few words: '*Knowledge of Purpose.*' You can't have a strong identity and be insecure at the same time. One weakens the other."

"Ah!" *Joy* nodded, because he had already scheduled a meeting with *Purpose* for the coming week. He felt enthusiastic about that future meeting, knowing now that he would definitely be arranging a replacement for *Insecurity*. *Joy* thanked *Insecurity* for the information and assured her that the world would be seeing less of her.

21

Joy Meets *Rejection*

It is better to follow even the shadow of the best than to remain content with the worst. And those who would see wonderful things must often be ready to travel alone.
—*Henry Van Dyke*

*J*oy thought seriously about not meeting with *Rejection*. "How about that?" he laughed to himself. "I'm actually thinking about rejecting *Rejection*!" *Joy* had experienced so much rejection already, he didn't think he needed much more. However, *Joy* also knew he needed to survey all the *Joy Robbers* to ensure they would stop stealing his clients.

When the two met, *Joy* reached out to shake *Rejection's* hand, but *Rejection's* body language told him that *Rejection* was not willing to shake hands. *Joy* shrugged and stepped back. In spite of *Rejection's* rudeness, he had to let him know that everything was all right.

"I realize that you are just being true to form, *Rejection*," *Joy* said. "I just want to let you know that I am not going to let you steal any more of my clients. In fact, I'm on to what you're all about."

"If you know so much already, then why are you here?" *Rejection* asked.

"I want to get information from you and find out if you really know your stuff," *Joy* replied.

"Suit yourself," *Rejection* replied. "I am a master at joy-busting, a *Joy Robber* of superb and extraordinary ability. My clients experience me at some of the most critical times in their lives."

Joy took out his notepad and asked *Rejection* to continue with his job description.

"All of my clients need acceptance and approval. They are performance driven, and generally, they 'go with the flow,' as it were. My major responsibility to my clients is to make sure that they never experience true acceptance.

"Don't misunderstand! I can create daily rejection occurrences for them; however, I work on their minds and emotions so that even when they have not been physically rebuffed, they will think that they have been."

Now *Rejection* laughed cynically. "My job is such a mind game," he continued, "that it's really not that difficult. I get help every once in a while from *Low Self-esteem*. That's when my job is easiest. She feeds them so well! Of course, once my clients feel rejected, they act out the snub on others. I'm sure it's easy for you to see that I'm a powerful *Joy Robber*."

Joy listened attentively. Although he did not like Rejection, he respected his job knowledge. "What would put you out of business, *Rejection*?" he asked.

"That's a difficult question with a complex answer," *Rejection* warned *Joy*. "If my clients could understand *Purpose* at a deep level, they would never feel rejection because they would understand the meaning of their existence. Once clients understand their true identity, it is difficult for me to convince them to feel rejected.

"I'm sure you've heard this before, *Joy*. You have a big job, but you'll never be able to replace me as long as my clients continue to doubt who they are and why they are here on the earth. As long as they continue to doubt their design and their *Purpose*, they will continually be plagued with feelings of dismissal."

"I certainly appreciate the time you've given me, sir," *Joy* responded, "but I would definitely like to reject you by replacing you. You are dismissed."

22

Joy Meets *Celebration*

A man can succeed at almost anything for which he
has unlimited enthusiasm.
— *Charles Schwab*

Joy was delighted to receive an invitation to meet with
Celebration. He could hardly wait to meet with this *Joy Builder*
who had always supported him and had made sure to always be at
their mutual events. *Celebration* opened the door and enthusiastically
ushered *Joy* into his seat in the living room. The guest suite was ready
for him, *Celebration* told *Joy*, concluding with: "And may I remind
you that you are just like a member of the family?"

"Thank you," said *Joy*. "Now I suppose you'd like to hear about
the assignment I've been on. It's important to both of us, I believe. I
am trying to protect my existing client base while moving clients away
from the competition over at *Joy Robbers, Inc.*"

Celebration nodded thoughtfully. "My own clients are becoming
quite savvy these days," he said. "A lot of them aren't waiting for an
important event to celebrate anymore, you know. They're beginning
to celebrate even the small things in life on a daily basis. It's keeping
me wonderfully busy, and I'm glad about it."

"No kidding!" exclaimed *Joy*. "I'm so happy for you!"

"Thanks, good buddy," *Celebration* replied. "Recently I've found
more of these clients rejoicing in their small victories and making

sure they maintained 'an attitude of gratitude' for their accomplishments in life.

"They are full of laughter and are learning not to take themselves so seriously. It's great! Some of my clients," he added, laughing, "get up in the morning and declare the entire day a celebration. What a terrific concept! I've been trying to spread the concept to all my clients."

Joy was almost speechless with admiration for *Celebration's* good work. "There's no question that I'll continue to work closely with you, because we're important to each other's success."

"Well, *Joy,* I need you to be there with my clients, too. In fact, you are the reason they do business with me in the first place," *Celebration* replied.

"I think we should celebrate our renewed and successful partnership," *Joy* said. "How about it? I want to show my appreciation and celebrate your wonderful work."

"Hurray!" exulted *Celebration,* jumping up and down and turning cartwheels. "It's celebration time!"

"Sure, throw a party, celebrate life," *Joy* laughed. "You can provide your guests with some 'Oats to Joy,' my fabulous oatmeal cookies, like no others you have ever tasted! Here you are," *Joy* continued, opening his briefcase. I promise you that your mouth will experience the flavor of joy."

Celebration, practically swooning with anticipation, suddenly realized that *Joy* had just taught him to continually find various simple tools for jubilation. As he imagined the taste of those cookies, *Celebration* understood this was an important lesson.

23

Joy Meets *Encouragement*

There are two ways of spreading light; to be the candle,
or the mirror that reflects it.
—*Edith Wharton*

Refreshed by the meeting with *Celebration*, *Joy* decided that since
he was in the neighborhood, he should go across the street and
see *Encouragement*. *Joy* didn't think *Encouragement* would mind his
dropping by unannounced, and he was right. *Encouragement* was
pleased *Joy* had stopped by. After all, he and *Joy* had been longtime
partners and knew each other well.

"Hey, *Joy*! It's always good to see you!" *Encouragement*
exclaimed, giving *Joy* an enthusiastic pat on the back. "I saw what
you did for my clients yesterday," he added. "I just want to
remind you what good work you do and how important you are
to all of us!"

"Man, I really needed to hear that," *Joy* responded gratefully. "I've
been working with some of the *Joy Robbers*, and the work has been
utterly draining."

"You never have to doubt how needed you are, because I am here
to tell you that if you weren't around, many of my clients would stop
doing business with me," *Encouragement* answered. "While I have
to admit that lately I've seen a slight decrease in my client numbers, I
am still optimistic that the numbers will grow this year."

"That's wonderful!" *Joy* replied. "But what is it that makes you expect your numbers to increase? What have you got going?"

"More of my clients are opening up to my new and improved *Universal Encouragement Training Program* as a way to serve them. They are beginning to realize that I've been right when I told them that encouragement is not just needed when you are not meeting your goal; even when goals are met, encouragement can help take clients to the next goal, the next level."

"Your new and improved *Universal Encouragement Training Program*? Sounds interesting," commented *Joy*. "Tell me more about it."

"As you probably know, everyone needs encouragement at some time in their life. Also," *Encouragement* continued, "my clients had thought that when the people around them wore a poker face that it meant they didn't want to hear kind words of encouragement. I've worked hard to change that perception. When my clients finally learn to give encouragement to their most difficult challenges, they are amazed at the positive response they receive.

"You know, *Joy*, some people have believed that I am only needed for women; this has been an ongoing problem for everyone, because male clients need me just as much as female clients. I think I became a gender issue because of male versus female communication problems.

"Anyway," he continued, "when I reviewed my female client list, I realized that many of them had not learned how to give positive encouragement to the men in their lives in a way that men can gladly accept and relate to."

"I think I know what you mean," *Joy* interjected. "Some men take the encouragement as condescending, or even confrontational. I've seen that happen many times."

"And of course, men need to recognize that encouragement and positive support are needed by the women in their lives, likewise delivered in ways that women find acceptable. Everyone needs me! My point is this: we still have work to do with our clients, but I believe it will continually improve," *Encouragement* concluded.

"You're probably right about that. Since men and women communicate differently to each other, they might perceive messages of encouragement from the opposite gender in a manner that was not intended at all!" *Joy* answered.

"Precisely," said *Encouragement*. "May I inspire you to review my new and improved *Universal Encouragement Training Program*? I have a copy of it right here. I encourage you to take it home and look at it. I'll bet you'll jump for joy after you see it! I'm sure your Joy program can benefit from it, too!"

24

Joy Meets *Positive Attitude*

You can complain because roses have thorns, or
you can rejoice because thorns have roses.
— *Ziggy*

*J*oy knew this neighborhood well, after having constantly spent time
here. He also knew *Positive Attitude* had one of the largest homes
on the block. He wanted to stop by his good friend and supporter's
place and bring him up to date on what he'd been doing. He rang the
doorbell, which chimed out the song "Accentuate the Positive."

"Hey, hey!" exclaimed *Positive Attitude* happily when he opened
his front door. Giving *Joy* a series of robust back slaps, he added, "It's
a great day whenever you show up, *Joy*! You know how much we
appreciate you here."

"Oh, I'm just making my rounds, trying to learn more about my
clients so I can develop better ways to serve them," *Joy* replied,
extending his hand. "I've decided to move in on the *Joy Robbers'*
business and capture as many of their clients as I can, which you
know will result in more referrals for you."

Accepting the handshake, *Positive Attitude* blissfully responded,
"No such thing as too much work for me, *Joy*, so bring it on! Thank
you so much!" He invited *Joy* to sit out on the patio, where he could
continue working on his jigsaw puzzle while *Joy* interviewed him.

They sat down at the patio table, where a main section of the puzzle had been completed. The remaining pieces were scattered about the table, haphazardly surrounding the main portion, waiting to be found and placed in their correct positions.

Joy asked *Positive Attitude* the usual question. "What do you think will bring you more clients?"

Positive Attitude smiled and said, "My clients must always remember I'm not a circumstance. I am a choice, so I can be there when they want me to." Finding the correct puzzle piece for an area he'd been working on, he continued, "They also should always remember that I am there to help them reach their goals. Without me, you see, they will hinder their success and the success of others."

Joy, who had been watching *Positive Attitude* as he talked and put together the puzzle, starting helping him sort the pieces. "So how does all that result in the growth of your client base?" *Joy* asked him.

"Well, *Joy*, I like to think that I am essential; however, for those willing to settle for mediocrity, I guess I'm not needed. I just hope that every day my clients will realize the benefits they have in front of them."

He found another piece and fitted it into the almost-completed puzzle. "I know *Trouble*," *Positive Attitude* continued, "and I've worked closely with him. He'll tell you that when we work together, our clients have done some really wonderful things to change the world."

"Really!" said *Joy*, handing him another one of the puzzle pieces. "What would you say about that, as long as I'm here and talking with you, *Positive Attitude*?"

"There's a famous doctor, Dr. Seligman, who's done a lot to help people in this area. My clients should take Dr. Seligman's advice and develop a method to dispute negative thoughts. They must fight off helpless pessimism." *Positive Attitude* continued, "Dr. Seligman's counsel is to argue with yourself, which has the effect of energizing you, making you feel ready to take on the problem. Viewing your situation logically and objectively can help you build a case against your pessimistic self."

Joy smiled and said, "I like the good doctor's advice." Continuing on that thought pattern, he asked, "Is it hard work to remain positive?"

Positive Attitude reflected a moment and then responded, "Since it's worthwhile, it's definitely a fight!" Moving more of the puzzle pieces into place, he continued, "It's a good fight, however, and it's won in the hallways of my client's thinking. My clients are always moving toward their most dominant thinking."

Positive Attitude suddenly let out a gleeful whoop. "We've got it! We're through with the puzzle! Happiness is mine! Thank you so much for helping, *Joy!*"

"Great!" answered *Joy.* "What is it?"

"It's my organization's vision and mission statement!"

AS A MAN THINKS, SO HE BECOMES.

"So true," *Joy* commented, as he examined the finished piece. "The power you have, *Positive Attitude*, clearly demonstrates itself when your clients choose to include you in their lives, as opposed to negativity and pessimism.

"When your clients think positively, good things generally have a better chance to happen. When clients think negatively, generally things don't turn out as well, anyway. That's a really good mission statement your organization has there," *Joy* concluded.

As he left, *Joy* thanked *Positive Attitude* again for all he had done to help make the world a better place, and said he would continue making his rounds.

25

Joy Meets *Love*

The love you share with you
is the love you share with others.
—*Sandra Steen*

Each time *Joy* had ever met with *Love*, he always felt as if he were entering *Love's* own little kingdom. *Joy* was reminiscing about the place where *Love* lives. Not too large, not too small, yet he had not seen all of it. Surrounded by a freeform wall of sturdy, fibrous-looking material, cherubs peeked playfully from its caverns and recesses. He recalled that her place had several chambers, and they all led to one particular chamber that glowed with amazing radiance.

Joy always looked forward to seeing *Love*, because she was always so understanding, so kind, so patient. *Love* never kept a record of his mistakes. *Joy* remembered the time he was late showing up for one of *Love's* clients, and *Love* just told him they would work through it. Fondly, he remembered *Love* explaining to him that "love covers a multitude of faults."

Love had a romantic side for her clients, but she was so all-encompassing in her approach that once her clients were stricken, they felt affixed to her at all times. With *Love*, it was a fact that most could not escape her, and most didn't want to.

When *Joy* pulled up, *Love* ran out with open arms to hug and welcome him. "You've come at just the right time, Joy!" she exclaimed happily. "I was just about to begin my cardiovascular workout for the day. Now you can join me! It's so much more fun when you have someone to do it with!"

"Uh-oh!" responded *Joy*. "Just what does that entail? What are you going to make me do?"

"Oh, don't be so silly! We're just going to do a little stair climbing and power walking through my house. It won't take long, and it'll add years to your life," *Love* replied.

"Now, *Love*, don't kill me with kindness. I'm pretty sure I can keep up with you. But I'd like to talk business with you during our workout. I'm visiting you because I want to find a way to get more clients for you."

"Great!" replied *Love*. "Come on, let's go. As you know, my house has four chambers, but we should start out in one of the two main hallways. Which of the two atriums in my house do you want to start out in, the left or the right?"

"Ladies' choice, my dear *Love*. Lead the way," *Joy* offered gallantly.

Love headed up to the right atrium of her house, her power-walk stride carrying her up the stairs with an even beat. *Joy* sprinted to catch up with her.

"*Love*, another reason I'm here is to make sure that the *Joy Robbers* won't have further opportunities to steal your clients," *Joy* panted as he caught up with her.

Love replied, "You don't have to be concerned, *Joy*, because God is Love and He will never be defeated. God is the ultimate Love, and the manifestation of His great love was His Son, Jesus. So, remember that Love cannot be considered only as an ideology, principle, or religious belief. Love is truth and it will never move. I know we always want the best for each other, you and I, and we will always protect each other. Together we'll persevere, because that's what we're all about." Her rhythm remained even, her breathing still regular.

They raced through the right atrium, crossing a partition that opened into the left atrium of *Love's* home.

"Let's take these stairs down to the lower chambers. We can stop and pump iron in the downstairs chamber here on the left side of the house, okay?" *Love* suggested.

"Fine," *Joy* gasped, wiping perspiration from his brow. "But getting back to the reason I came here, how do you think we can do more for our clients?" he asked.

Love thought a moment as they loped down the stairs and into the lower left chamber. She grabbed a set of tubular-shaped weights and handed them to *Joy*. "Start lifting," she commanded. Then she continued, "Our clients must understand that love is what they ultimately do for themselves and from themselves. They must also choose to love all kinds at all times. We aren't options, but rather a constant choice.

"Of course, *Joy*, there are people who are difficult to love, but what good are we if we are just helping our clients love the people who are easy to love? You have to have the kind of love that circumstances cannot change. My clients know that they may love from a distance, but that is better than not loving at all.

"When choosing the people you walk with, it is not mandated that you walk with everyone that you have chosen to love. Love can exist among people who do not share a kindred spirit. In fact," *Love* continued, pumping iron with measured effort, "there are some people my clients have to learn to 'love them alone.'"

Joy smiled, despite the heaviness of the weights. He knew exactly what she was talking about. In fact, *Joy* himself occasionally had to "love some people alone." This reminded him of *Love's* tough side, the one she uses for discipline. She would often say that she loves her clients too much to leave them the same.

"Why don't we move on to the next chamber now, *Love*? I've had all the fun I can take with these weights," *Joy* pleaded. Without waiting for her response, he headed towards the partition to the lower chamber on the right. Hoping to find a bench where he could sit for a moment and collect his breath, he was instead greeted by the sight of a large punching bag that hung from the ceiling, supported by a network of valves and pipes of some sort.

Coming up from behind him, *Love* put on a pair of boxing gloves and began addressing the punching bag. One-two, one-two, one-two, she thumped. Luv tuff, luv tuff, luv tuff. Every time *Love's* fist hit the bag, that sound seemed to fill her entire house, the 'luv' long and low pitched, the 'tuff' snapping and high pitched.

"I serve my clients in a variety of complex ways," *Love* stated as she continued punching the bag, "and just about everyone is able to understand my universal importance. Even the *Joy Robbers* understand this."

Joy joined *Love* at the punching bag. "Yes," he observed, "but the *Joy Robbers* steal your clients by making them confuse love with control, obsession, selfishness, and a host of other bad and unloving behaviors."

"I know, *Joy*, I know. But my clients, when they choose *True Love*, elect to speak and live and give in *Truth*. They recognize that their true power is in controlling themselves only, not in controlling their loved ones; they speak kindly, or they don't speak at all; they give generously, and from the heart. They know that jealousy and obsession with the object of their love are bad things. The *Joy Robbers* don't have a prayer with those particular clients!"

Their workout done, *Love* and *Joy* headed back up the stairs, where *Love* invited him to relax in her special hot tub and spa. Tired and aching all over, *Joy* gladly accepted. The hot tub was located in his favorite room of the house, the one filled with the glowing and amazing radiance he had recalled on his way over. The tub itself—fed by what seemed like hundreds of pipes, tubes, arteries, and valves— was immense. It was so large that seeing beyond it was like trying to see past an ocean that never ends.

Joy slipped gratefully into the tub. Closing his eyes, he submerged himself completely for a moment in perfect enjoyment of the warm waters that rushed to meet his face, his hair, his essence. *Joy's* meeting with *Love* underscored to him the big job that still lay ahead, and he was happy knowing that he and *Love* were on the same side.

Joy told *Love* how much he admired and appreciated her.

26

Joy Meets *Hope*

If hope does not spring eternal, then something else will.
—*Sandra Steen*

*J*oy was so inspired by his meeting with *Love*, he decided to keep going along his positive path and stop to check on *Hope*. He thought to himself, "How do I depict or explain *Hope*? Her job description is so massive! She works so closely with *Love* that it's hard to separate the two."

He looked to see if *Hope* was home, knowing she was always there, but *Joy* thought it would be important to check. *Hope* answered the door wearing bright colors and a beautiful smile. *Joy* told her he was in the neighborhood and just wanted to stop by to let her know how his mission had been going.

Hope looked puzzled. "Come on in and sit down. What new ventures are you involved in?" she asked *Joy*. *Hope* appeared somewhat anxious by this, because she knew *Joy* had plenty to do just working with his own clients.

Joy replied, "I've decided to increase my clientele, and I'm working on new partnerships to help replace the *Joy Robbers*. This is important work, *Hope*, and I'm committed to seeing upward changes in the joy levels of the world."

Hope smiled. "Our partnership is firm. My clients have always welcomed you, and I appreciate your work. I'll do all I can to support your efforts."

"Excellent!" exclaimed *Joy*. "So, where do I tell my clients that they can find you? Your own work is so important that everyone needs to know of a place where they can be sure you'll be there."

Hope nodded, understanding exactly what *Joy* was asking. "I will always be found in the mind of my clients," she answered. "They simply have to believe that I exist. If my clients believe this, they will wait patiently for me.

"You don't need hope for what you already have, for one thing. And *Joy*, for another thing, if you always lead your clients to the place they expect me to be, then I will always be there."

Joy, thunderstruck with the simplicity of *Hope's* explanation, said, "I just realized, *Hope*, that you are the embodiment of the philosophical adage 'I think; therefore, I am'! I know you've told me about your job function several times before, but this is the first time I've truly understood it. If your clients use their mental capacities to call upon you, even just thinking you may be there, well, there you are! Completely within reach!"

"Exactly," answered Hope. "I can be there for anyone and everyone. They just have to say the words 'I hope.'"

"I must get the word out then, *Hope*, because a lot of my clients have looked for you in the wrong places."

Grateful for this meeting and thanking *Hope* for her time and insights, *Joy* left, hopeful that he could get the word out quickly to the clients that were looking for her.

27

Joy Meets *Faith*

The end of the matter with God is always good;
if it is not good, it is not the end of the matter.
—*Sandra Steen*

Although daylight was racing to its finish line, *Joy* was too inspired and elated not to continue his quest. "You don't talk to *Love* and *Hope* and miss the opportunity to meet with *Faith*," he told himself. First, *Joy* called *Faith* on the phone, knowing that she was always busy working on a new project. He told *Faith* he was around the corner and wanted to visit with her for a short while to discuss how they could both increase their workload. *Faith*, though busy, said she'd be delighted to see *Joy*, since they had worked together for many years.

Joy arrived at *Faith's* place and observed that her desk was covered with her clients' plans and projects, all kinds of blueprints, proposals, bids, and other documents. *Faith* rifled through them and then displayed her clients' dream sheets for *Joy* to examine.

"I keep records of my clients' hopes and dreams," she explained, "so that I can supply them with enough 'substance so they can continue to hope.' I can't give them hard evidence of what is about to happen for them, but I need to supply them lots of energy to keep working in the direction of their dreams."

"How does faith come to your clients?" *Joy* asked.

"*Faith* comes when my clients hear the words spoken by God," she replied, smiling.

Joy was fascinated. Everywhere he looked, he saw evidence of matters that *Faith's* clients believed in, despite the fact that whatever these things were, they had not yet taken place.

"I'm curious," *Joy* said to *Faith*. "What happens to your clients when their lists of requests go unfulfilled?"

"That never happens," *Faith* replied.

"Oh, come now. Wait just one minute, *Faith!*" *Joy* objected vociferously. "You can't tell me that every single little or big thing your client believes will happen actually does happen!"

"'Oh you of little faith!'" she replied, half mocking him. "Everything is granted to my clients according to their faith. You'd better get your notebook out and start writing all this down."

"Of course, of course. Thank you," said *Joy*.

"Let me explain it to you like this. If you are applying for a loan and you fill out the application, there are required fields that you must complete. The application is your statement of faith. If your loan request was denied because the information was not complete," *Faith* continued, "your request was not rejected. You simply did not meet all the required conditions to be approved, because your statement of faith was incomplete. You did not meet all the conditions required.

"Of course, in this case, because you are realistic about the amount for which you can qualify and you meet the credit and income requirements, you could resubmit your application with the complete information and be approved."

Joy smiled and replied, "I hear what you're saying. You are simply stating that sometimes your clients submit incomplete applications, and then they need to resubmit their applications completely filled out—their complete statement of faith."

Faith nodded and replied "There are always conditions that must be met. Understand that my clients cannot live without complete faith, and without me in total and complete form, they cannot please God.

So you see, *Joy*, at the end of the day it's not how complete your wish list is, it's how complete your faith is."

Joy was amazed but perplexed, because *Faith* had to play the double role of providing her clients something concrete and something very abstract. "How does she do all that?" he asked himself. "What I do is so much simpler than what *Faith* does."

"How do you get your clients, *Faith*?" *Joy* asked, poised with his pen and notebook.

"I get my clients from the people who have the need to trust something more than what they see with their eyes," she replied. "An example I can give you is that of persons suffering from cancer. They can't see those cancer cells growing and mutating, but they see and feel the destruction of their bodies.

"In some cases, however, when their faith is strong enough and they apply their faith completely through both proper medical care and prayer, they can go into remission. They can't see the cancer cells disappearing, but they know the cells are gone. That's faith working: their faith in the Lord, their medical practitioners, and themselves."

Joy smiled. "I get it," he said, his bewilderment suddenly going away. He wrote a little more.

"*Joy*, you need to remind your clients that if they have faith but take no action," *Faith* continued, "then I have to leave. I only activate my power when my clients take action in the direction of their beliefs. This is how their faith is made complete."

Marveling at the sudden clarity with which everything was coming together, *Joy* jumped up with his pen and notebook. "*Faith*, this meeting has been nothing but splendid. Now I'm certain that we will both continue increasing our client numbers."

Faith smiled, pleased. "*Joy*, I know you'll always hold on to the faith!" she exclaimed, laughing.

28

Joy Meets *Vision*

Vision without action is a daydream.
Action without vision is a nightmare.
—*Unknown*

*J*oy needed to move on quickly now, because he did not want to be late for his meeting with *Vision*. They were scheduled to meet in a conference room on the twenty-third floor of the high-rise building where *Vision* resided on the same floor. Unfailingly well dressed and articulate, *Vision* was always ready to look into the future with everyone who asked him to. *Joy* looked forward to this meeting, because he always learned so much when he talked to *Vision*.

Vision entered the room and gave *Joy* a firm handshake. "Welcome to the future!" he said cordially.

"Thank you, I appreciate your giving me your time," said *Joy*. "Let me tell you why I've come to see you. I'm in the process of creating a new vision for my organization. Part of this process has been to get more clients through stronger partnerships with the *Joy Builders*. But I also want to look past the present with my clients to ensure that the *Joy Robbers* won't have continuing opportunity to destroy their lives, as in the past.

Vision nodded, impressed with *Joy's* strategy.

"Tell you what, *Joy*. Let's go out to the balcony, where I have a telescope set up for stargazing. It's a beautiful night tonight, and we should be able to see quite a few stars, and maybe even Venus or Mars. We can enjoy the splendid view of the city lights below, too."

"I get it. You go out there and look at all those stars and planets, light years away, and you're really peering into the future, right?" observed *Joy*.

"Well, it's the past, really," *Vision* answered. "It takes thousands of years for the light they emit to travel over to Earth and hit the telescope lens so we can see them. But if you think in terms of getting over to those other planets and stars some day to explore more of God's creation, then yes, it is the future, indeed."

They stepped out onto the balcony, where *Vision* began adjusting and focusing the telescope lens.

"So how can I help you with your objectives?" he asked.

"Well, I would like to know how I can partner with your clients by bringing them joy at the same time that you bring them vision," *Joy* replied.

"Here, take the telescope and look at the moon. It's gorgeous tonight, and the stars look like sequins on velvet. The way I see it, just as in looking through this telescope, I show them their future, or tomorrow's view, as it rides on the light of the past." *Vision* said.

Then he continued, "Actually, *Joy*, yours and mine is an easy partnership, because without me my clients will die on the inside. I provide them with views of their possible futures, and *Faith* and *Hope* both work closely with me to keep the engine running. Your job is to make sure that their hearts are glad as they look and see the good things that are still to come.

"You see, I provide the planning process for my clients; but you, *Joy*, can provide the emotional process for them. It's a beautiful partnership and I know it can work well."

Vision took hold of the telescope tube. "So how does everything look out there? Do you have a good view of the stars and the moon? Do you think you can see tomorrow?" *Vision* quizzed.

"I have a splendid view of everything, *Vision*, thank you," *Joy* answered, returning the telescope to him. "I understand what you mean now by looking into the future in the light from the past. The light of the past is really the lessons your clients have learned from their mistakes as well as their successes."

"Exactly."

"So how do your clients get started with you?" *Joy* wanted to know.

Vision replied, "I couldn't happen for them without my clients going to *Hope* and *Faith* first. After they've done that, then I need them to write me, their *Vision*, as a statement, so that I'm clear to everyone. I should be written describing the impact I will have on the lives of others. Once that is done, everyone who reads about me should be able to achieve me over time." *Vision* snapped the lens cover shut on the telescope, and they walked back inside the conference room.

"*Vision*, this is going to be a very smooth operation," *Joy* said. "Now I can see how I can bring more joy to your clients. I can't wait to get started—in fact, I'll provide you with a vision statement in writing as soon as I can. This was a most informative interview. And thanks for the light show. My vision is clear now."

"And I'd like to thank you for your follow-up and commitment to excellence," *Vision* replied. "I see bright horizons in your future."

29

Joy Meets *Patience*

My promise is in need of my patience;
my patience is in need of my promise.
—*Sandra Steen*

Joy realized after interviewing *Hope*, *Faith*, and *Vision* that he had better understand more about their mutual friend *Patience*, who seemed important in their lives. When he arrived at *Patience's* address, 1777 Everlasting Avenue, it seemed to take forever just to get up to the front door. The long, winding driveway made it even more time-consuming: *Joy* counted three traffic lights on the driveway, each with a red light lasting at least five minutes, and the corresponding green light flashing on for no more than five seconds. There was even a school crossing. It's not that he minded waiting for the children to get by—they were all so cute, happy to be out of school for the day, their colorful backpacks bouncing up and down from their shoulders as they skipped to the other side of the road.

After the last child skipped by, *Joy* drove forward, only to come to a duck crossing—and he was still only in the driveway. *Joy's* teeth began to clench, his knuckles going white on the steering wheel as he watched the mother duck hovering over her little ducklings as they ambled all over the road to get to the other side.

Once *Joy* finally made it to the front door, it took *Patience* forever to open it, or so it seemed. He began to wonder if *Patience* was trying his patience.

"I hope this meeting won't be like my trip up the driveway," *Joy* thought to himself. He shook hands with *Patience* and said, "I'm here to get some information from you to see how you and I might work together on my plan to replace some *Joy Robbers*. I'm hoping that you and I can be effective partners in this project."

"Mmm-hmm," *Patience* answered, nodding slowly. He was silent for a moment and then said, "Let me explain, *Joy*, that you shouldn't expect to understand me or my function in just one meeting. I believe it will probably take several meetings and some time before you can truly understand what it is I do for my clients. Not because I think you're less than intelligent, but because what I do is more complex than most people even realize."

Feeling frustrated now because his schedule was being squeezed, *Joy* nodded quickly to acknowledge that he understood. He began to wonder if he would have the time that *Patience* appeared to require.

Now *Patience* was smiling. "Today is your lucky day, *Joy!*" he exclaimed with enthusiasm. "My siblings are all here for our annual family embroidery contest. We're embroidering the world's biggest tablecloth. We'll be using various techniques, including the plaited stitch, the Italian hemstitch, the stem stitch, and various others. It will be such fun for you to watch, don't you think? And you can practice your patience while you're at it!"

"Umm, ah, I really need to get on to some of my other clients, *Patience*," was the unenthusiastic response. "Maybe I should get back to you after your embroidery contest is over."

"Nonsense! I won't hear of it! You must come and watch! In fact, you won't just watch—we'll let you participate! Here is your needle and thread, and you should sit next to my sister *Endura* and help her with her end of the tablecloth," *Patience* said, patting the chair next to his complacent-faced sister.

Resigned to learning about embroidery and the virtues of being patient, *Joy* took his place beside *Endura*, who smiled pleasantly at him.

"Let me tell you about how we do the plaited stitch." *Patience* continued talking, oblivious to *Joy's* anguish. "First, we lay vertical threads close together across an embroidery hoop. Then we work from right to left, weaving the needle over and under three or four of the foundation threads, keeping an even stitch. 'A stitch in time saves nine,' as we always say, eh, *Joy*? Now, the Italian hemstitch is a bit different ..."

"*Patience*, why don't you tell me about your responsibilities while we work on your tablecloth?" *Joy* interrupted purposefully.

Seeming not to notice *Joy's* anxiety, *Patience* complied and began an unhurried explanation of his duties. Each word seemed to be measured. "Essentially, *Joy*, I provide the fuel that steadies my clients so that they can maintain their cool and self-control while awaiting an anticipated end.

"You see, if my clients can't wait and try to get ahead of me, they will generally create only counterfeit dreams, having left me behind. However, if they are more patient and work with me, they will indeed find the real thing, their real dream.

"But if they bolt past me without waiting to examine the issues with more care, they generally find that they were conned by an impersonator to reach their anticipated end. That end usually turns out not to be the end they really anticipated in the first place. 'Good things come to those who wait.' Surely you've heard that saying before."

"Of course, of course," *Joy* answered quickly. He was feeling antsy now, hearing about all of this waiting business, and he chided himself for being so impatient. "Tell me something, as I'm curious," he said. "Where do your clients find you?"

"They find me in the vision or the hope they believe in," *Patience* responded, after a lull filled in with stitching. "If you know what you believe in and it hasn't happened yet, then you wait on it and trust that it will happen. Eventually."

"Ouch!" *Joy* exclaimed suddenly. "I stuck myself with the needle. Oh, it hurts!"

"Patience, patience, my good friend. Endura will get you a bandage. Just take your stitches a little more slowly now until you've acquired the experience and confidence to move more quickly."

"Lesson learned. Thank you," *Joy* replied. "You were telling me about your clients' hopes and visions and how these relate to having patience. Do go on, *Patience*! I'd like to hear more about that."

Another pause. Stitch, stitch, stitch, stitch. *Joy* waited expectantly, needle poised.

"Let me explain, then." *Patience* continued stitching. "My clients don't wait on a vision by simply standing or sitting around and doing nothing. Waiting is an action, much like that of waiters or waitresses who wait on their customers, ready to be of service to them as soon as their customers decide what to ask for." A quick whip, a finished stitch from *Patience*.

"Finally!" thought *Joy*. "The information I need! And it looks like we're finishing this end of the tablecloth, too. Thank God."

Patience continued, "Waiting, then, is an action of service and it is there where my clients will find their patience. I encourage my clients to find me by serving others."

"You know, *Patience*, this is good stuff you're telling me," *Joy* responded. "I wonder how much publicity would be needed to get you some more clients. So many of my clients say they don't have patience, and that they don't want to pray for it. Can you explain why this is?"

A moment of silence. Of course. More stitching.

"The reason your clients don't want to pray for patience is because when they do, *Trouble* comes," *Patience* answered. "I know you've met with *Trouble*, and I'm sure you understand how *Trouble* can bring on impatience and stress for those who don't want to exercise me on their own.

"It's best to calmly wait for a positive outcome or result without being hasty or too impulsive. If you have a quiet confidence in God, you have no need for being anxious. If you can operate without fear or stress, knowing that your vision and goals will come, you can have *Patience* with no problems."

Patience stopped talking. Clarity came at last to *Joy*. He was thrilled, having realized that by tolerantly waiting and listening to *Patience*, he had reached his reward, the information he'd been seeking.

"*Patience*," *Joy* said, "I'll need your help to get through waiting for my next meeting with you, even while I know that in the end I'll be glad I was patient. In fact, I know that I can get started on the 'patience' part of my project just from the information you've given me today."

Unhurriedly, *Patience* responded, "I tell my clients that they must always remember that the race of life is not given to the strong or the swift, but to those who will endure to the end. *Joy*, because of your endurance, I want to congratulate you on receiving what you came for. And because of this, you won't need to have a whole string of meetings with me—well, perhaps only one more." *Patience* smiled at him.

"Wonderful!" *Joy* replied. "That's such good news, because I really need to move on with my assignment. I couldn't ask for a better reward. Thank you, *Patience*! I look forward to working with your clients."

As *Joy* began moving towards the door, *Patience* said: "Tell you what, *Joy*. Believe it or not, we finished embroidering the tablecloth during our meeting, and my family and I would like you to have it as a gift and a reward for your patience."

Endura and her sisters and brothers brought the tablecloth to Joy, unfolding it for a view of their handiwork. In exquisite and colorful embroidered stroke stitch, surrounded by equally exquisite embroidered flowers, were the words:

"How Joyful Is My Patience."

Joy beamed with pleasure. "Oh," he gasped, "it's so incredibly beautiful! This has been one of the most satisfying experiences I've ever had. Thank you, *Patience*, for showing me the way!"

30

Joy Meets *Appreciation*

The deepest principle in human nature is the
craving to be appreciated.
—*William James*

*J*oy had almost forgotten about his meeting with *Appreciation*
because it was so easy to take her for granted. Unassuming and
humble, her power could be lost on one's consciousness. She was
powerful because she worked with her clients to keep them aware of
the positive things in their lives. Her clients projected what was
described as an "attitude of gratitude." They radiated a positive effect
on those that surrounded them. *Joy* was glad he did not take
Appreciation for granted, because he knew she had important clients
for him.

When *Appreciation* arrived, she immediately thanked *Joy* for his
time and told him how much she appreciated what he was doing.
"I'm so glad that someone's taking the initiative to do something about
the *Joy Robbers*," *Appreciation* said to him, "and I'll do all I can to
help with your project."

"Thank you," *Joy* replied appreciatively. "It's such a gorgeous
day today! Let's go out and walk in the park while we talk. Are you
up to it?" he suggested.

"Absolutely," was *Appreciation's* enthusiastic reply. "I just love walking park-side trails, seeing all the gorgeous wildflowers, walking in the cool shade of the trees, and all that neat stuff!"

"I didn't know you were such a nature-girl!" *Joy* teased.

"I just like everything that the world is made of," *Appreciation* answered, her smile as radiant as the sun.

Together they made their way to a nearby park and found a quiet trail that ran alongside a stream, the water making the only noise as it ran and splashed over stones and under bridges formed by vines and other flora.

"You seem to know about my project already," *Joy* began. "Who've you been talking to?"

"Oh, I talk to *Positive Self–esteem* and *Positive Attitude* almost every day, and they told me about it. I hope that's all right with you, *Joy!*" *Appreciation* answered.

"Of course it is," Joy replied appreciatively. I guess everyone's getting on board with this. Then you probably already know that I want to learn more about your techniques and procedures to support your clients, because I also want to do more for them."

Appreciation closed her eyes and thought a moment. Then she began explaining. "I represent an outlook—or a perspective—on any and all things in life." She stopped and picked a cattail from its cluster in the nearby stream. The cattail flower was in bloom, its green leaves waving prettily in an exotic dance with the wind.

"The perspective that I bring to my clients allows them to create a positive focus. Here, let me show you." Holding the cattail in one hand, *Appreciation* reached into her pocket and pulled out a magnifying glass. "It's like looking at this cattail with my magnifier. Did you know that cattails are imperfect flowers?"

"No, I didn't," replied *Joy*. "But where are you going with this?"

"I'm creating a positive focus on something that's less than perfect. This cattail probably won't win any beauty contests, although when its flowers enlarge, they become those long brown spikes that some people use to decorate their homes in the wintertime," *Appreciation* answered.

"Really! So that's what they are! I never knew that! I've always liked those displays of long, brown grasses in those big vases," *Joy* replied. "But I'm a bit puzzled with your analogy. Why is this cattail less than perfect?"

"Aha! Because cattails are among the imperfect flowers, which have a calyx and a corolla, but either have no stamens or have no pistils. Perfect flowers, like roses and lilies, have stamens and pistils — and a calyx and corolla."

"So where and how does the appreciation play in?" queried *Joy*, still puzzled.

"Simply by the fact that although this flower is imperfect, as are people, it still has a bloom of its own, and it still carries out many functions. Besides being used for winter decorating, cattails also provide a silky down that is used to dress wounds and also for upholstering. Bet you didn't know *that*!" *Appreciation* concluded exuberantly.

Joy laughed. "No, I certainly didn't. And now I have a new appreciation for the humble cattail."

"Good," said *Appreciation*. "I have succeeded in getting you to appreciate this most unassuming of flowers. Now, to expand upon my role just a bit more, my clients understand that whatever they focus on takes on size, sometimes a life of its own. Just like when we were looking at this simple cattail and appreciating its function despite its being an imperfect flower. We appreciate the modest cattail for what it is, and we give thanks to our Creator for giving us something to decorate our homes with, something with which to dress the wounds of the injured, and something to stuff our sofas with."

"I get it!" exclaimed *Joy*, truly happy to finally understand what *Appreciation* was trying to tell him.

"So when I consult with my clients," she continued, "they begin to view their lives with 'an attitude of gratitude.' They can be found thanking someone for something done for them, whether great or small. They also enjoy practicing 'random acts of kindness.'

"My clients believe that they should give flowers to people while they can still smell them. I have never quite understood why some people wait to show appreciation for someone who is lying in a casket. My clients understand that every day presents a new and wonderful opportunity to be appreciative."

Joy nodded his head. "That's a good point," he said. "Now I can see clearly why your clients can experience me with no problems." He picked a wild rose from the side of the trail and handed it to *Appreciation*. "For you," he said. "A perfect flower. Know that I am always at your service."

Appreciation smiled and accepted the flower with sheer delight. "How sweet of you," she commented.

Joy replied, "A servant's heart, I have found, is always full of joy. It's amazing to me that more people don't seek this incredible form of joy."

They continued down the wooded trail, following the stream that meandered through the park. "You know, *Joy*, a lot of people do eventually find me," *Appreciation* said. "However," she continued, "my job is to help them discover the gift of appreciation before a bad situation creates their worst memories."

"I'm not sure I follow," *Joy* replied.

"Well, then," *Appreciation* continued by asking, "perhaps you've heard the saying 'You don't miss your water until your well runs dry.'"

"Sure! I have ancient clients who use to say that all the time," replied *Joy*.

"Well, if people are taking something or someone for granted, they will often discover appreciation once that something or someone is missing. And that can be so tragic. So, perhaps now you can see why I am so passionate about helping them discover their gift of appreciation before a bad situation forces them to that discovery."

"Oh, I get it," said *Joy*. "The gift of appreciation. You help your clients uncover it. How marvelous! I really want to see you get more clients, too. Your work is so important to the human spirit, and I so appreciate you for it. I'll continue spreading the word to some of my other partners about your wonderful gift. I'm sure we'll send you lots of referrals."

"You know I appreciate that," she answered. "But there's something else, too, that helps my clients discover their gift of appreciation. It's the simplest thing, yet no one seems to consider it until it's suggested to them by someone else. It's almost like it's a secret that doesn't want to be one."

"Sounds intriguing," *Joy* answered. "Well, I'm stumped. I don't know what this secret is. Tell me, tell me!"

Appreciation laughed with delight. "You'll kick yourself if you haven't thought of it before, *Joy*," she said. "You know how people make their 'wish lists' all the time? 'I wish I had this, I wish I had that'?"

"Sure," said *Joy*. "That's sort of like a motivator, if it's not misused as a 'gimme' list. A wish list can give you an objective to work for if it's used properly."

"Well, what if people made an appreciation list, too?" *Appreciation* ventured. "They would list the things they are grateful for and that they appreciate. 'I appreciate Mom and Dad and everything they did for me; I appreciate this gift of a beautiful day today; I appreciate my economics teacher for trying to make the subject interesting'—you know, like that!"

Joy stopped in his tracks. Slapping himself on the forehead, he said, "Now, why didn't I think of that? Of course, *Appreciation*! That's a marvelous idea and a quick way for clients to discover—and care for—their gift of appreciation. Because once you discover what you appreciate, you care for it by expressing thanks or enacting some other form of gratitude."

"You got it!" *Appreciation* replied. She smiled happily.

They headed back to *Joy's* place in silence, appreciating the natural beauty that surrounded them as well as each other's company.

As she was leaving, *Appreciation* smiled slightly, saying, "Wait a minute, Joy." She stopped and began writing something down on a piece of paper. *Joy* waited as she completed her thoughts. "I have something special for you," she said.

Intrigued, *Joy* waited patiently as *Appreciation* searched in her handbag for whatever it was. Then she found it. Smiling even more, she handed *Joy* a beautiful bookmark, artfully embossed with lace and dried violets. With it was an envelope with *Joy's* name on it. He became even more intrigued as he opened the envelope. Inside he found a card of thanks that read:

To *Joy*:
Thank you for all the joy you bring, and may it return to you daily a hundred fold.
Sincerely,
Appreciation

Delighted with her thoughtful gesture, *Joy* gave *Appreciation* a big hug. It was so nice to be appreciated.

31

Joy Meets *Purpose*

Each of us comes into the world with an
assignment to fulfill.
— *Myles Munroe*

*J*oy was feeling overwhelmed by the enormous amount of
information he had acquired from all of his visits. Still, he knew
that with all of that data, he was going to be able to make a difference
in the lives of his clients. He also realized what a big team project this
was becoming.

Joy began looking over his notes and writing down his plans to
expand his operation, determined that with the help of his friends, he
could meet all of his goals. As he reviewed his notes, *Joy* remembered
many of his clients referring to *Purpose* as significant in their lives.

Joy decided he was ready to interview *Purpose* and find out how
he could best serve his clients. Despite his feelings of preparedness,
Joy was feeling a little nervous about meeting with *Purpose*. He had
such high regard for *Purpose* that the very idea of sitting and talking
with him was daunting. He knew from experience that *Purpose's*
clients kept him very busy, and thus he had not had the opportunity
to meet with *Purpose*. This was a really big deal for *Joy*. He knew this
would be a defining moment for himself and his clients.

It was time. From the window, *Joy* could see *Purpose* surrounded by *Vision, Hope,* and *Faith.* It appeared they were in a meeting of their own. Joy walked in and greeted everyone, telling *Vision, Hope,* and *Faith* that it was good to see them again.

"Take a load off, *Joy,*" *Purpose* said cordially, inviting him to take a seat. "We're just wrapping up our meeting. We've been here all morning talking about how to increase success for our clients."

Joy was thrilled upon hearing this. "Maybe I'm the one who inspired their meeting," he thought to himself.

The group chatted pleasantly for a little while, and then *Vision, Hope,* and *Faith* left to pursue their own endeavors. Now *Purpose* looked at *Joy* intently, and it appeared to *Joy* that he had a lot on his mind. "*Joy,* I'd like you to know that indeed you are an important part of my clients' success," he said.

"And I would like you to know that I appreciate your time. I know it's valuable, and I won't take up a whole lot of it," *Joy* responded.

"Nonsense," *Purpose* replied. "It's my pleasure to meet with you, and I don't consider it an interruption."

"All right," said *Joy,* beginning the interview. "Can you tell me where you have come from?" *Joy* felt like a little child trying to understand one of the Wonders of the World.

Purpose smiled at *Joy,* pleased by his question. "I come from the mind and the heart of the Creator. And I come from the mind and the heart of the creator."

"Umm, *Purpose,* did I hear you say the same thing twice?" *Joy* asked. He wondered if he was hearing an echo.

"Yes and no, *Joy,*" replied *Purpose.* "Let me try to explain. Our clients, being creations of God, have a responsibility to live for and know their Creator. He created our clients—and us—for His own purposes. Those purposes of God's are part of a larger scheme that He has planned for everyone, for all of eternity.

"Purpose is not about the self-directed questions most people ask, such as 'Why am I here, or 'What is the reason for my past being what it is?' In fact, purpose is about God's grand design for the entire universe, of which we—our clients, and you and I—are just one part. To say this another way, then, I do not come at all from within my clients, but rather from deep within the heart of the Father, Creator of all things. He knew what His purposes were for us before we even took our first baby breaths."

"That is astounding!" *Joy* exclaimed. "Then, it seems to me, that our clients have to be close to God to even begin to comprehend what the purpose is for anything, right?"

"Yes. We may not quite understand His purposes for us, but they are from deep within His heart," replied *Purpose*. "His purposes for us are personal, and they are specific to each of us. Purpose is not really about our clients, or about us, *Joy*, like so many people tend to think. Purpose starts and ends with the source of all life, which is God."

"So you're saying that 'purpose' is known only by the one who creates something, right?" interjected *Joy*. He continued, "Purpose doesn't come from me, because I didn't create myself; it comes from the One who created me; in fact, from the heart and the mind of my Creator, right?"

"I do believe you understand, *Joy*," *Purpose* answered.

"This is so profound, *Purpose*," uttered *Joy*. "Based on what you've just said, I think I have better insight of my own personal relationship with God and His purposes for me. But you mentioned the word 'creator' twice when we started this conversation. Tell me about that one."

"Okay," *Purpose* said agreeably. "I have an idea. I'd like to show you what I mean by saying 'creator' twice the way I did earlier. We'll go in your car. I've always liked your *Joy Rider*. It looks like a lot of fun."

Off they went, the *Joy Rider* cruising smoothly and uninterrupted along the coastal highway until they reached their destination, the convention center building in downtown Point City.

"Okay, I must say I'm intrigued," *Joy* told *Purpose*. "Why are we here?"

"You're in for a treat, *Joy*, and I'm going to let you figure it all out," replied *Purpose* with a grin. "Today, the Kitchen Sink Trade Show just happens to be going on, and I'd like you to 'check it out,' as they say these days."

"A 'Kitchen Sink' Trade Show?" *Joy* asked incredulously.

"Well, they really mean 'everything but the kitchen sink,'" *Purpose* laughed. "Come on! Let's go on in!"

In they went. It was indeed, "everything but the kitchen sink." Hundreds of booths lined the grand room of the convention center. The noise was a magnificent mix of music, laughter, and the hum of a thousand gizmos being hawked by their hopeful vendors. There were dancing girls, singing choirs, accordion troupes, posters, banners, balloons, videos, and PowerPoint presentations, all exuberantly presenting the glories and promises of the products the sponsors were exhibiting and selling.

"Wow!" *Joy* remarked. "I wonder if this was what it was like when Jesus went into the temple that time and threw everyone out!"

They walked alongside the rows of booths, stopping here and there to look at one thing, see how another thing worked, and to accept free samples of products from the pretty young girls and handsome young men who represented the manufacturers and importers. They turned the corner, and there, seemingly isolated from the other vendors, was a gray-haired, bespectacled woman sitting quietly in her booth, her hands folded peacefully in her lap. There were no signs, no banners, no balloons, no posters, no videos, no dancing girls, none of the hoopla that surrounded the other booths. Instead, on the counter and on some shelves behind her were clear bottles and jars, about one-quarter filled with a colorful, grainy substance, and tightly sealed.

"Good afternoon, gentlemen," the woman said greeting them.

"Good afternoon, ma'am," *Joy* responded politely.

"Feel free to look closely at my product," the woman offered. "I'll be happy to answer any questions you have."

Purpose, true to his word, stepped back to let *Joy* begin his inquiry and his adventure in discovering purpose.

"What are these jars and bottles you have here?" *Joy* asked the woman.

"I'll give you three guesses," she replied, handing him one of the jars. "What do you think they are?"

"Hmm, let's see," *Joy* said, musing aloud and turning the jar over and around to examine it. "My three guesses are: upholstery cleaner, or bath salts perhaps, or maybe some kind of health-food powder to mix with water or milk?"

"That's a 'no' on all counts, I'm afraid," replied the woman. "This is an invention of mine, which I hope can eventually solve the problem of world hunger."

"This little jar with this sandy-looking stuff in it?" *Joy* responded incredulously. "You think it will cure world hunger? I have to hear about this!"

"To you it may just be sand in a little jar, but this is actually powdered water. To get it to liquefy, all you do is add air, and presto! Water! Two parts hydrogen, one part oxygen." She stopped talking and waited for his reaction, which came immediately.

"Oh, my gosh, this is amazing!" exclaimed *Joy*, turning excitedly to *Purpose*, who was standing there watching the discovery adventure unfold. "Isn't this the most amazing thing you ever saw?" *Joy* asked him.

He turned back to the woman and said: "You're right about the possibilities of solving the world hunger problem. This is light, portable, you could probably pack it in even lighter hermetically-sealed plastic packages, and you could transport it for relatively little money to the parts of the world that are suffering from drought."

"Exactly!" replied the inventor, joining *Joy* in his excitement. "I'm also developing a method that can load the powdered water into irrigation systems, so that as the powder shoots out, it turns into water as soon as it hits the air. Think of what this can do for farmers! Think what this can do for cities having problems with their water resources! And even if all you want to do is a little hiking or backpacking into the woods, this is much lighter to carry than several canteens of water."

"Ma'am, I am astonished by this invention of yours and the importance of your work," *Joy* said to her. "But you need to get the word out! Where are all your signs, your banners and balloons?"

"My intention is to focus directly on the production of the powdered water," the inventor answered. "It's my belief that my invention will carry itself to transform the world. I fail to see how banners and balloons will get this product to the places where it's needed."

"And I thought you were selling bath salts!" said *Joy*. "I'm so glad I asked you what your intentions are." He turned to *Purpose* and said, "Now I know what you mean by purpose being in the mind and heart of its creator."

"I think our boy *Joy* has got it!" *Purpose* announced triumphantly, to no one in particular. "You've developed a relationship with this inventor, and you've discovered her purpose for what she created."

As they left, *Joy* again asked *Purpose* about his function and the relationships he creates with "creators" and "the Creator." "I just want to be certain that I fully understand your meaning."

"Let's talk about 'the Creator' first," *Purpose* replied. "It's the 'Creator' who directs the lives of his creations. The lives of all His creatures are in His power. So, it's vital to get to know the Creator intimately and have a personal relationship with Him."

"And the other 'creator' is any one of your clients," *Joy* interjected. "Just regular, ordinary people who make their own decisions about how to live their lives, whom to marry, what career to pursue, what new gizmo to invent, what new book to write, and things like that. But only their 'Creator' knows the divine purposes He had for them when he first created them." *Joy* finished.

"Exactly, exactly!" *Purpose* exclaimed.

"So how is it that so many of your clients are discovering their purpose?" *Joy* asked.

"You see, creators—whether they are inventors of lifesaving apparatus or inventors of new tuna casserole recipes—know what they want before they create, and their plans are predestined. At the same time, however, those who fail to make contact with their own

Creator fail to make contact with their real purpose. It is only when they connect with God—then and only then—that they can find, read, and understand the legend for their personal blueprints and understand their true purpose."

"I think I understand the way you work more clearly now," said *Joy*.

Purpose smiled. "It helps if you understand that someone's purpose begins and ends with 'the Creator,' with God Himself. Even one of the world's most famous philosophers, who happened to be an atheist, said that unless a God is assumed, the question about life's purpose has no meaning.

"My clients have awakened to the fact that everything has a reason for its existence. We may not know all the reasons, since they reside in the Creator's heart.

"Now, *Joy*, with regard to many of my clients: as you can see now, they are also creators, although of course, they aren't God. I help them understand that putting together the smallest or grandest item, and knowing why they do so, is a reflection of God's purpose for them. This inspires them not just in their thinking about the purposes of their own creations, but also of the Divine Purpose that God has for them. Their search for me is ongoing, because I am complex and comprise many elements. My clients understand that they don't just simply arrive at their purpose. They continually explore and grow in the knowledge of its many facets."

"What happens next, after your clients discover their purpose?" *Joy* wanted to know.

"Then they devise a plan for their purpose, and the plan defines their performance. This keeps them drawing and filling in the various 'rooms' on their blueprints. They look at the whole design and figure out why they are here." *Purpose* replied.

"What more do you think I can do for my clients, once they have discovered their purpose?" *Joy* asked.

"Just continue being there," *Purpose* answered him. "One of the most joyous of occasions for my clients is when they find me through developing their relationship with God. They begin to understand that they are part of a much grander scheme for the purposes of God. When that happens, it's as if a burden has been lifted from their lives. Where they couldn't earlier find peace, contentment, and order in their lives, with me there—and with you there—at last they have it all. So, please, *Joy*—just stay put."

"Not a problem, *Purpose*. It will be my pleasure to remain close to you and your clients," *Joy* said as he got up to leave.

"Oh, by the way, don't forget to talk to *Peace*," *Purpose* told *Joy* as he walked him to the door. "*Peace* lives next door to me, and we collaborate on lots of projects. Many of my clients seem to find *Peace* as a result of finding me, *Purpose*."

"Now I'm really clear on why your clients always seem to find you, *Purpose*. Thanks for the information," *Joy* said as he smiled and waved goodbye. "You've given me a great deal to think about. It's great having a partner like you."

32

Joy Meets *Arrogance*

For everyone who exalts himself shall be humbled,
and he who humbles himself shall be exalted.
— *Luke 18:14*

As it turned out, *Peace* wasn't in. "There must be a purpose for his not being here and my having to come back some other time," *Joy* thought to himself as he headed home. "Maybe *Peace* is over in a war zone trying to prevent the loss of lives."

When he got home, *Joy* looked at the list of *Joy Robbers* and *Joy Builders* whom he still needed to interview. He decided to pick up the phone and schedule an appointment with *Arrogance*. "Might as well get this unpleasant session over with," *Joy* muttered to himself as he listened to the telephone line making the connection.

When *Arrogance* answered, "The *Arrogance* residence, *Arrogance* speaking. This had better be good," *Joy* gave a perfunctory greeting after taking a moment to recover from the sting of *Arrogance's* rude greeting. Then he proceeded with the purpose of his call.

"Hmmph," sniffed *Arrogance* haughtily. "I wish insignificant peddlers wouldn't waste my time calling me at home with their useless projects. I'm far too important to play tiddly-winks with commoners like yourself." Then *Arrogance* hung up on him.

Joy, infuriated with *Arrogance's* show of complete disrespect, decided to drive to his house and confront him personally. The drive was a long way from where *Joy* lived; he rarely traveled to this part of the world. He knew he had to go a long distance down Pride Avenue, and he had been told he would make a right on Lack of Humility Boulevard. *Arrogance* lived on the corner.

As *Joy* drove over to *Arrogance's* house, he realized he was making a bold move. This was the same man who had just hung up on him. Would *Arrogance* add a finishing touch by slamming the door in *Joy's* face? "It doesn't matter if he does," *Joy* thought to himself. "This is an important assignment, and I'm not afraid of him."

He rang the bell, which chimed to the song "You're So Vain." *Arrogance* answered the door and immediately asked, "Who are you?"

Joy replied, "I'm *Joy*, the one that you hung up on a few minutes ago. I just thought I'd come by so that we can be properly introduced to one another."

"I don't need an introduction to you," *Arrogance* told *Joy*. "Everyone knows who I am, and that's all that matters. I'm *Arrogance*, and you're not. Why don't you go play in traffic, or something?"

Astounded by the magnitude of self-importance displayed by this *Joy Robber*, *Joy* replied, "Actually, I'm here on a critically important assignment, which you happen to be a part of."

"Important?" *Arrogance* repeated. "Well, then, your assignment must be about me. Come in, then," he said gruffly, holding the door open for *Joy*.

"That's a good clue," *Joy* thought to himself as he entered the front hallway. "As long as *Arrogance* thinks that my mission is important and all about him, he'll talk to me. And since he loves to talk about himself, I'll find out everything I need to know."

Arrogance ushered *Joy* to the den at the back of the house, where he promptly sat in an overstuffed recliner and lit up a big cigar. *Joy* sat on the sofa.

"So, *Joy*," *Arrogance* began, speaking through small puffs of the cigar. "I happen to be so good at my job that you're not needed around here. My clients don't need you or anybody else, for that matter. I'll be glad to tell you about how great my work is, so if you're not here to talk about me, you can just leave." He flicked the ashes from the cigar into a trophy cup that served as an ashtray. His likeness was engraved on the cup.

"Of course this is about you, *Arrogance,*" *Joy* replied, playing up to his host's oversized ego. Then he thought silently to himself, "I'm just not telling you that it's also about me and all the *Joy Builders.*"

"Well, your mission must be important if you're here to see me," *Arrogance* growled, "but as I just said, no one here needs you. I don't need you, either." He started blowing smoke rings that billowed lazily in the air.

"Hold on, *Arrogance,*" *Joy* countered. "You can't mean that your clients don't need anyone. Everybody needs somebody at some point in their lives."

"Well, *Joy,* you're wrong when it comes to my clients," *Arrogance* answered, puffing and blowing more smoke rings. "My clients represent the best and the brightest in the world. They're not your average Joes—they're the most educated, they have the highest IQ's, and they solve problems for the rest of the feeble-minded world. So, I told you, they don't need anybody!"

"I find that very interesting, *Arrogance,*" *Joy* responded. "Let me ask you this: where did your clients get all of their knowledge?"

Gazing down his nose at *Joy, Arrogance* replied, "They attended the greatest educational institutions available."

"So they were taught by those who were taught, and that means they needed someone to get where they are," *Joy* said.

"Look," *Arrogance* replied testily. "My clients aren't interested in you, *Joy.* They are interested in *Power.* Being happy is not what produces *Power.* For my clients, knowledge is *Power,* and I simply don't think you have anything to offer to me or my clients." He chewed on the cigar, then started puffing more smoke rings.

"I respect the intellectual capacity of your clients," *Joy* told *Arrogance.* "But may I ask you what would have to happen for you to lose a client?"

Taken by surprise with this question, *Arrogance* settled down for a moment. "You know, I've never been asked that question before," he said, chewing on the cigar tip. "And I have to admit that I love a good challenge. I will do anything and everything to keep from losing clients.

"But to answer your question, I could probably lose clients if they went through a humiliating or tragic event in their lives after having been on top of the world. I've had clients who've gone through some really rough changes after being caught doing something unethical or experiencing great losses that were beyond their control," *Arrogance* continued. "And then they discovered that they had alienated so many people while they were top dog, they had very few friends left. I've noticed that after this, I don't see them around the *Arrogance* chambers much anymore."

Joy answered, "I sure hope your clients will find use for me before they have to experience 'a great fall.' It sounds as if your clients may think more highly of themselves than they should. You know, *Arrogance*, conceit is always too high of an opinion, and when conceit comes down, it falls awfully hard. And the self-absorption displayed by conceit does nothing to soften the fall."

Arrogance was quiet for a few moments, and then realizing he'd been out of character, jumped up. In an aggressive tone, he told *Joy*, "Say what you want—it doesn't matter. For the last time, I'm not interested in you or what you have to say. You're not the answer for my clients, and I'm not doing business with you."

"You may think you're strong," *Joy* countered evenly, but I have strong partners who I know will cooperate with me in every way to get you replaced. I have more influence than you think."

"Hah!" snorted *Arrogance*. Now he was standing directly in front of *Joy*, and he blew a smoke ring directly into *Joy's* face, laughing.

"*Arrogance*," said *Joy* calmly as the hazy circle floated lazily around his face. "I think you blow a lot of smoke."

Arrogance stopped laughing. His eyes narrowed, and he slowly took the cigar out of his mouth. "What? What did you say to me?" His teeth were clenched in anger.

"I said that I think you blow a lot of smoke. You can take it any way you like."

Stunned at *Joy's* confidence, *Arrogance* could say nothing. He'd spent the entire interview talking tough, singing his own praises, and he'd actually blown smoke in *Joy's* face. He hated being outsmarted like this.

Collecting himself, *Arrogance* replied, "I see you are confident and prepared; however, you have no rank. Have your CEO call me, and maybe I'll look at your plan.

"I never deal with such a low-level employee like yourself. Here's my card. Have your boss call me. No, have him call my secretary to arrange a meeting."

Joy smiled as he left. While his boss resisted the proud and the arrogant, he knew that if *Arrogance* wanted a meeting, he would surely get one.

33

Joy Meets *Charity*

This only is charity, to do all that we can.
—*John Donne*

J oy had invited *Charity* to lunch and found himself captivated by her beauty. "She is so lovely," he thought to himself, "this will not be my last meeting with such a stunning individual as *Charity*."

Charity was warm and friendly, and she acknowledged everyone in the restaurant, giving each of them a small gift that she seemed to have readily available. She studied the people around her, appearing to have a sense of those in need. She was relaxed, poising herself gently so that she could easily respond if someone asked for help.

An elderly woman seated near *Charity* seemed to be having trouble getting out of her chair, and *Charity* was there instantly to make sure she got up safely. *Joy* observed that *Charity* did not seem to care about race, creed, or color as she looked with openness to offer support and a helping hand.

Charity began the conversation by thanking *Joy* for inviting her to lunch. "I always enjoy working with you," she said smiling, her face glowing with happiness. "Without you, I don't know how I could continually inspire my clients," *Charity* added.

"I feel the same way," *Joy* replied, and continued, "I hope that our partnership will inspire others."

Across the restaurant, a customer raised his voice. He could be heard by everyone as he berated his youthful server. "I know how to make chicken a la king. In fact, I can make it for you. I asked how *you* make it here at this restaurant, but it seems to me that you don't know. You should find a job sweeping floors or something, if you don't know how to answer a simple question about the menu."

"Oh, dear," *Charity* murmured. "I see a future client right in front of us."

The young server tearfully fled the dining area, and the loud, obnoxious customer threw his napkin down and left the restaurant in a huff. *Arrogance* could be seen following right behind, smirking.

"Oh, no, him again! Of course!" *Charity* exclaimed. "Why else would that customer treat that poor young waitress so poorly? Well, I'll have to catch up with them later. Sorry to have digressed from our interview, *Joy*. Go ahead, I'm listening."

"*Charity*, you are such an inspiration! How are you doing these days? Are you getting more clients?"

"Well, we both just saw one who got away! But seriously, I am always getting more clients, but it's never enough." She paused for a sip of water. "I mean, when you think about all of mankind serving one another, you know the possibilities are endless. So, although I always get more clients, I still always need more clients."

"Well, *Charity*, I have some good news. My goal is to do more for you and increase my presence with your clients. With me pumping all that joy into them, perhaps that will inspire them to refer others to you."

"Thank you, *Joy*, that's wonderful," replied *Charity*. "I sure like the sound of that. You know who I miss?"

"No, I don't," replied *Joy*, intrigued.

"I miss some of my star clients, and I most especially miss Mother Teresa."

"Indeed," *Joy* concurred. "That's easy to understand. Mother Teresa was in herself the very definition of charity and selfless love for all of humanity, no matter how humble, how sick, how poor. She was amazing."

"I have one of her quotes with me in my World Impact Journal, where I keep an account of my clients' good thoughts and generous actions," *Charity* said, pulling an attractive, leather-bound notebook from her handbag. "Let me read the quote to you:

'Life is an opportunity, benefit from it. Life is a beauty, admire it. Life is a dream, realize it. Life is a challenge, meet it. Life is a duty, complete it. Life is a game, play it. Life is a promise, fulfill it. Life is sorrow, overcome it. Life is a song, sing it. Life is a struggle, accept it. Life is a tragedy, confront it. Life is an adventure, dare it. Life is luck, make it. Life is life, fight for it.'

"Wasn't she just fabulous?" *Charity* enthused, as she browsed through her journal.

"She covered it all, didn't she?" *Joy* responded.

"Ooohhh! Here's another one of my clients in my World Impact Journal that I miss tremendously — Martin Luther King, Jr.!" *Charity* said with both excitement and regret. "He was certainly a champion for charity across the world."

"His 'I Have a Dream' speech was powerful and carried such impact," commented *Joy*. "It continues to influence the lives of many of my clients, even today. Mother Teresa and Martin Luther King, Jr., are what I call *World Changers*. What other quotes do you have from him in your World Impact Journal?"

Charity read aloud, "'Everybody can be great, because anybody can serve. You do not have to have a college degree to serve. You do not have to make your subject and verb agree to serve. You only need a heart full of grace. A soul generated by love.' He had it so right, *Joy*!" *Charity* sighed audibly and put away her journal.

"Actually, I have some other wonderful clients, and they're doing a good job of making charity a worldwide practice," *Charity* continued. "You and I must continue to show our clients the rewards of practicing charity, and in doing so, I know that service to one another will continue," *Charity* concluded.

"Yes, yes! I believe that!" *Joy* shouted, happy beyond description with *Charity's* commitment to their partnership. Everyone in the restaurant turned and stared. Slightly embarrassed, he silently thought to himself, "I couldn't be the only one who recognizes the inner and outer beauty of wonderful *Charity*."

"Tell you what," *Charity* said. "I really think we should get our partnership strategy down in writing. I have an idea. Let's make it a little contest. We'll both list as many potential client contributions as we can think of, and the one who lists the most gets lunch paid for by the other. Come on! How about it, *Joy*?" *Charity* challenged him, smiling.

"*Charity*, you're so clever!" *Joy* answered. "What's great about our partnership is that when you bring people's charitable services to the needy, I show up as their joy. All right! On your mark, get set, go!"

They both started scribbling furiously on their napkins. After a few minutes, they both put their pens down at the same time. They compared notes. Then they both laughed. "Looks like it'll be Dutch treat today," *Joy* remarked. "We are the best of partners, indeed."

They had both listed:

1. Build job skills programs for the unskilled.
2. Promote adult literacy.
3. Provide services for coping with sudden job loss.
4. Provide assistance for victims of natural disasters.
5. Give aid to victims of violence and abuse.
6. Take care of widows, orphans, and the elderly.
7. Provide medicine and medical services to the sick and disadvantaged.
8. Distribute clothing to the needy.
9. Help create shelter for the homeless.
10. Feed the hungry.

"Just think of the joy our clients will feel when they receive the help they so desperately need," *Charity* said softly.

Joy smiled, adding, "Just think of all the joy our clients will receive when they give the support that is needed."

"Indeed," they both said to one another.

34

Joy Meets *Choice*

You cannot escape influences. They are there for you to allow or
refuse, choose or reject. What you decide about them
will determine your character.
A man is what he chooses to be.
—*St. Augustine*

Today *Joy* was meeting with the one he thought of as "everyone's engine"—*Choice*. His plan was to influence her clients to vote for him, *Joy*, in their daily decisions on how they would feel about life in general. "Choose *Joy*!" would be his campaign slogan. *Joy* understood that *Choice's* clients voted with their emotions on a daily basis, and he just wanted to make sure he was always on the ballot.

Choice walked in and immediately gave *Joy* several options of where they could sit. She then gave him options on what they might talk about, and then she gave him options on taking handwritten notes or videotaping their meeting. When *Joy* chose to continue with his usual handwritten notes, *Choice* gave options among pens and pencils of different colors.

In just a short while, *Joy* began to feel decision anxiety. "My clients must be going through this daily with the *Joy Robbers* and the *Joy Builders*. I'll bet it gets to be really challenging," *Joy* thought to himself.

He asked *Choice* what she does for her clients. *Choice* replied, "Do you want the long or the short answer?"

"I'd prefer it if you just choose what you think is appropriate as we go along," *Joy* replied. He could feel his patience being tested. "Having too many miniscule decisions to make can be overwhelming, especially if you have to agonize about options in life that don't really change anything," he mused to himself.

"Okay, thank you, *Joy*," said *Choice*. "I just love choosing everything." Then she continued, "I maintain my clients' *Personal Will*. I make sure that their *Personal Will* is not violated."

"I don't understand what you mean by 'personal will,' *Choice*. Can you clarify that?" *Joy* asked.

"I mean that my clients are empowered to exercise free will when they make the choices in their lives. No one should interfere with that, but sadly, when *Joy Robbers* like *Control, Fear, and Intimidation* come around, they sometimes make my clients believe that they don't have the free will God gave them when they were born."

"That's a tough crowd to have to deal with," commented *Joy*. "I can understand why you sometimes have trouble getting your clients to recognize that they really do have the right to make their own decisions. Of course, they may not feel that way if someone is making them feel guilty or obligated. Positive influences that lead to good decision-making is important, but arm-twisting manipulation does not qualify in this category."

Choice responded, "Someone who chooses to violate every tenet of God's plan for my clients is a threat to their future. The most important capability that I give my clients is the opportunity to weigh the consequences of their choices. When my clients look at their lifestyles, they will also see the abundance in their choices."

"I don't mean the smaller choices that don't impact one's life, for example, deciding whether to use cold water or warm water when they wash their clothes. I'm talking about the choices and decisions that may alter the course of their lives and the lives of those around them."

"Do you mean that when they come to the proverbial 'fork in the road,'" *Joy* interjected, "that you help them recognize that making a good choice usually brings good consequences? But making a bad choice always brings bad consequences—if not sooner, then later?"

"Exactly," *Choice* answered. "Without knowing that equation, and that they do have options, they would never understand why and how to choose what's good for them."

"It almost seems like a formula for life that you're offering to them," remarked *Joy*. "Making a good choice equals getting good results; making a bad choice equals getting bad results."

"You're right, *Joy*," *Choice* answered, smiling. "My clients understand that good and evil coexist, and that they have the option to choose between them." *Choice* continued, "It is amazing to me that God Himself allows my clients to choose between good and evil. It remains very important to realize that if God protects the *Personal Will* of my clients, everyone else should.

"I am always cheering for my clients, hoping that they choose the good; unfortunately, I have clients who don't listen to me and make the wrong choices."

"Then what causes your clients to make those wrong choices?" *Joy* wondered aloud.

"Sometimes my clients are influenced by *Manipulation*, a major tool of *Selfishness*. When he gets to my clients, he uses various deceptive practices to get them to choose something that will allow *Selfishness* to get her way."

Joy had heard of *Manipulation*, but he was unfamiliar with his work. "Can you tell me something about him?" he asked *Choice*.

"*Manipulation* and *Selfishness* team up often, and together they produce a selfish agenda in which they find ways to get my clients to choose what's in their own best interests, but not my clients'. It can sometimes seem harmless, but it's in violation of *Personal Will*, and I work hard to stop it."

"I've met with *Selfishness* already and have been strategizing about ways to handle her. How do you believe I can produce more joy for your clients when *Manipulation* is hanging around, too?" *Joy* asked *Choice*.

"When my clients aren't looking for 'the big event,' but are exercising a daily practice of good choices, then I believe they will experience joy. Even when my clients make bad choices, they can still experience you."

"Really!" *Joy* exclaimed. "How is that?"

"They learn from their mistakes, and when they realize that they've finally learned the lesson that was presented, they experience joy!" *Choice* replied.

"Of course! I knew that!" *Joy* responded. "I was just testing you, *Choice*."

"Do you really think I'll choose to believe that?" *Choice* teased. Then she continued, "My clients know that they're earning a Ph.D. in experience, and my job is to make sure they don't flunk out. When I lose clients who have not learned the lessons of life, they start believing that they can no longer make decisions. They stop making active, personal, and specific choices, and they then start living their lives by default. You could almost say that it's like living life at random. The product of this lifestyle is uncertainty, and a by-product is often misery for my clients and the people who love them."

"I have no doubt, *Choice,* that my services are vital to your cause," *Joy* noted. "I'd like to continue to work with your clients by simply showing up as a reward for good and bad choices."

"That's the choice I would make," *Choice* responded, smiling. "Well, I have to run now. I have to go to a meeting where some votes are being recounted because my clients didn't like the outcome."

"I look forward to being a frequent choice for your clients," *Joy* said. "Please take some of my slogan bumper stickers with you to remind your clients to "Choose *Joy*!"

35

Joy Meets *Courage*

Courage is the greatest of all virtues,
because if you haven't courage, you may not have an opportunity
to use any of the others.
—*Samuel Johnson*

Joy looked at *Courage* with great admiration; after all, he wore a badge of honor and had an incredible presence coupled with strength. "This *Joy Builder* is vitally important to all of my clients," Joy thought to himself.

Joy reached out to shake hands with *Courage*, but then instead, he lifted his arm high to salute him. *Joy* couldn't help it. Saluting *Courage* just seemed to be the natural thing to do.

Courage graciously accepted the honor and thanked *Joy* for his time. "Our conversation should begin with my acknowledging the value that you bring to my mission, *Joy*," said *Courage*. Joy felt especially proud hearing this come from *Courage*.

"Thank you for your kind words," *Joy* said, beginning his interview. "Can you tell me where your clients find you, *Courage*?"

"They find me connected to their personal passion," *Courage* replied. "Often they find me when they are working on their commitment to others."

"And what is your responsibility to your clients?" *Joy* asked, as he pressed on with the interview.

Seeming eager to respond, *Courage* replied, "My responsibility is to help my clients manage fear while taking an appropriate action. I help them to desire safety while still taking the risks necessary to live life fully."

Courage continued, "My clients make the tough decision to continue, despite the obstacles. They understand that courage isn't based on an outcome, but rather is the basis for contentment."

Joy, impressed with *Courage's* job description, wondered aloud how he could be a part of this wonderful process. "So *Courage,*" he said, "how can I help your clients?"

"Just always be there when my clients have to make the tough decisions," was the reply. "I know you've met with *Choice,* and I believe together you and *Choice* can help my clients maintain their 'gladness of heart' in tough situations. Many of my clients serve their country or their communities by performing dangerous jobs daily. They know how important their sacrifice is to someone else, and they are also sober in realizing the serious threat to their personal safety."

Joy nodded and accepted the challenge; he knew how important this assignment could be to everyone. *Courage* continued, saying, "I'm always available to everyone that needs and desires me. I hope that more and more people will choose me. I would love to see my client list grow from last year."

"We'll make that happen," *Joy* replied. He felt glad, knowing this would be an important alliance. *Joy* also knew that the *Joy Robbers* wouldn't stop because of the strength of *Courage*; but if he and *Courage* banded together, they could send the *Joy Robbers* packing.

Their alliance sealed, *Joy* saluted *Courage* again and thanked him for his time and the valuable service. *Courage* returned the salute and said, "You have a brave heart, *Joy*, in your willingness to go to some of the world's most dangerous places with me! I salute you!"

36

Joy Meets *Pain*

Suffering ceases to be suffering in some way
at the moment it finds meaning.
— *Victor Frankl*

Joy dreaded this particular meeting. Over the years, he had become acquainted with *Pain* through many clients he had lost to this perilous yet receptive *Joy Robber*. *Pain* was a complex operation, a curious mix of contradictions. *Joy* knew that the time had come to learn more about engaging with this sharp if not smart potential partner and client.

Dragging himself in on crutches, *Pain* lurched into the meeting room dressed in an array of somewhat artfully wrapped bandages, scabby edges of scars vividly exhibiting themselves in places the bandages didn't cover. *Joy* suspected there were even more of those scars hidden underneath the splintered trappings of gauze and muslin. He felt the intensity of *Pain's* presence the moment he entered the room; it was obvious that *Pain's* burden was heavy, although *Joy* could not visibly distinguish it.

Joy thanked *Pain* for pressing through his obvious discomfort to talk about his role with his clients and began the interview by expressing his interpretation of *Pain's* role in *Life*. "I see you as *Life's* dashboard of gauges, alerting your clients to both a deep revelation about their issues and a heightened sense of freedom.

"For example," *Joy* continued, "if a client develops intense pain, the pain becomes the driver that leads her to the doctor. When she gets to the doctor, her description of the pain becomes a way to lead the doctor to finding what ails her so that she can be healed. The source of the pain is revealed, and the doctor helps her free herself of it. In other words, pain leads the client and the doctor to the greater problem, which leads to the ultimate solution. *Pain,* does that make sense to you?"

Pain grimaced and then gazed, unblinking, at *Joy,* who immediately looked away. The silent anguish behind the eyes of *Pain* seemed to reach out, brushing *Joy's* own eyes with the stings of salt and sorrow. *Joy* braced himself to look back at *Pain,* now fully recognizing the power of both agonies brought on by physical and mental suffering.

Finally *Pain* spoke. "Yes, you are making sense, *Joy,*" he groaned, his eyes filling with tears. "I play a role in my clients' lives to let them find the deeper solution. Emotionally, I bring them to a point of such pain that it usually brings about a change in behavior."

Pain coughed and gasped, but continued. "As an example, the mother eagle uses great wisdom when she is teaching her babies to fly: she simply makes the nest so uncomfortable that they no longer want to be there. Their discomfort launches them into flight.

"Typically, my clients will not change what they have grown to tolerate, so I must take them beyond their level of comfort. When their pain comes," he continued, "several things can happen. My clients will first try to find ways to stop the pain. For the clients who pay attention, they eventually succeed at stopping the cause of the pain.

"In some cases, however, my clients will stop short of identifying what is causing their pain and simply seek to medicate it. Whether their pain is emotional or physical, this behavior can lead to abuses with drugs, alcohol, or other things."

Now more gasps and grimaces, and then *Pain* resumed. "A lot of times, I'll show up right before *Life's* birthing process, when the birthing of ideas or concepts is coming into fruition," he continued. "Perhaps you've heard the saying 'It is darkest before the dawn.' For many of my clients, right before the most magnificent change comes, they often experience their greatest pain. The pain I deliver can become so intense that often they want to give up rather than push to success.

"My female clients who've given birth to babies can relate to this. The process of physical pain and birthing is clearly understood by them. However, on an emotional or spiritual plane, the birthing process of a dream or a vision is not limited to females.

"*Joy*, I hope that you can get the point of this analogy. For example, at times, it can be agonizingly painful for any man or woman who is struggling with an idea, a decision, or a dilemma to bring it to its resolution. Until their ideas or decisions solidify and form completely, they cannot carry out the birthing process to its conclusion."

"I'd love an example of this pain-to-birthing process you're talking about," *Joy* interjected.

"Oh, my aching head," *Pain* commented. "Sometimes it hurts to even think. Just a moment, *Joy*, while I pop an aspirin, okay?"

Joy laughed and replied, "Do you really need an aspirin, *Pain*? You're here with me, *Joy*, you know!"

"Hmm, you're right," *Pain* answered, embarrassed. "Sometimes I get so focused on myself and what I'm feeling that I forget that I'm not the only person in the world or the center of the universe."

"You were about to give me an example of the pain-to-birthing process for difficult decisions or ideas," *Joy* reminded him.

"Okay. Let's take a career-making decision that involves the dreaded *M* word, *moving*. I have two clients, a married couple, Connie and Jeff. They have four children, they each have jobs, and they have a beautiful home on a river. Jeff has always told Connie that her career is top priority and that he will support her and do whatever it takes to help her advance in her company.

"Connie has worked hard and was recently selected for promotion. It's exciting for her, because not only does she feel rewarded for her dedicated work, it also requires moving to a beautiful city in the mountains. The company will pay all of her moving expenses and help them buy a new house, even larger and more beautiful than their present home. Her new salary and benefits will permit them to provide more for their children and will allow them luxuries they can't afford now."

"Doesn't sound painful to me at all," *Joy* commented.

"You're right, so far," *Pain* answered. "Connie was elated when she learned about her promotion from her boss. She swore that wings grew on her feet. But when she came home and announced the news to Jeff, he informed her that he wasn't moving out of their town. He gave her all sorts of reasons, none of which sounded like his initial promise to support her quest for growth in her career. However, Jeff told Connie she could take the position and move if she wanted to and that he wouldn't stop her, but he would have to divorce her if she did. But he said it would be an amicable divorce. He promised not to fight over custody or financial issues. This, in his own mind, was his attempt at being fair and equitable."

Stunned by this story and the painful decision that Connie was now required to make, *Joy* commented, "Incredible! No matter what path she takes, Connie will be meeting you, *Pain*. It's as if she's being punished for getting a promotion instead of being rewarded! So tell me, what's happening? What is she doing about this?"

"Well, she has to think about her children," *Pain* replied, "especially the little one. Finding appropriate day and nighttime care during her evening shifts is going to be a terrible problem. She would be moving hundreds of miles away from family and friends, you see, and would be truly alone, with no one to help her during times of illness or other crises. She also has to deal with her husband literally pulling the rug out from under her."

"And all along you're there with her, while she's deciding what to do, I suppose," remarked *Joy* sadly.

"Every minute of the way, *Joy*. I need to make certain she feels every bit of the highs of her promotion and the lows of being betrayed by her husband. I want to burn that contrast into her memory so that she never forgets the devastating power of promises that are broken.

"With this new and painful *Life* lesson that has been presented to her, she can make her decision: take the promotion and move alone with her children; or stay in her current and very boring job, with her family intact. With either decision—and the consequences of that decision—Connie gets me for company. I'm with her whether she stays or goes. You can't say I don't take care of my clients!"

"So can you tell me what's waiting for Connie when she makes her decision, whatever it is?" asked *Joy*.

"What I can tell you is that, whatever she decides, she will live with it and with me, *Joy*, until she resolves to push me out of the picture and bring you in. In accepting the consequences of her decision, she'll call on you to help her find renewal in her life. Who knows? Her joy could lie in keeping her family intact—or in kicking her husband to the curb for his betrayal and then managing on her own. I really don't know what she'll do at this point."

Joy crossed his arms. "You know," he began, deeply concerned for Connie, "sometimes it's hard to determine whether physical pain or emotional pain is the stronger. I have to say that this story of yours will be seen as quite sad in the eyes of some, although I suppose there are stories that are sadder and more painful."

"Indeed, there are. But *Joy*," *Pain* countered, "if my clients can push through their pain, most of them usually forget its intensity afterwards, because of what lies on the other side of that discomfort."

"Such as...?" *Joy* asked.

"Such as the calmness that comes after your decision has been made. Usually, there've been a storm of choices that were part of the decision, but once made, the decision gives you a direction to follow.

"Such as a beautiful child, God's special blessing, whose arrival may have been unplanned or unexpected. Or a beautiful dream, goal, or vision that has come full term. An example is Connie's promotion, which was a result of her hard work, independent study, and volunteerism.

"Such as declaring peace instead of declaring war. Such as resolving to live honestly and within your means, when it is so easy to live beyond your means in order to give others the impression that you are more successful than you really are. The list can go on forever. And in all, *Joy*, this whole problem with the pain of decision-making and its consequences is one great big paradox."

Inspired by *Pain's* comments, *Joy* had begun taking notes. "So how do you think you and I can work better together to resolve the paradox?" *Joy* asked.

"In my opinion, our partnership happens to be the essence of the paradox I just mentioned," *Pain* answered as he wrapped a new bandage around his swollen arm. Our slogan should be '*Joy* in *Pain*,' don't you think?" He smiled with excruciating difficulty.

"Really! And why is that?" *Joy* wanted to know.

"While I inspire change that leads to redemption from my clients' pain, you can protect their hearts from *Bitterness* and *Unforgiveness*. You know how those twins are always looking to get my clients," *Pain* replied.

"Oh, now I can see why you like that slogan," said *Joy*. "But I think that if I can somehow get through to your clients and provide an overall sense of future well-being, they won't have to do business with *Bitterness* or *Unforgiveness*, no matter how great the pain caused by a friend or family member or someone they trusted."

Pain, by now leaning forward, his hands clutched to his chest, said, "*Joy*, you know I was half-kidding a few minutes ago that our slogan should be '*Joy* in *Pain*.'"

"I know," *Joy* answered. "I'm sure you've heard it said that sometimes it takes feeling bad to know when you're feeling better."

"*Joy*," said *Pain* with some effort, "just your presence today has made me feel better, and I know you'll do the same for all of my clients. Thank you."

"You're welcome, *Pain*," he answered. "I look forward to doing more business with you. Of course, while I can't offer your clients a 'no-pain guarantee,' I am a state-of-the-art pain reliever. *Pain*," *Joy* added, "when you see her, please let Connie know that her weeping might endure through the night season, while you are with her. But then tell her that joy will come in the morning season when it's my turn to spend time with her."

Pain looked up at *Joy* now and thanked him without grimacing. Meeting his gaze, *Joy* did not look away.

37

Joy Meets *Drama*

The office of drama is to exercise,
possibly to exhaust, human emotions.
— *Laurence Olivier*

Joy could not quite figure out why he needed to meet with *Drama*, but he had been told that she was a real *Joy Robber*. He was baffled, because he had always thought *Drama* was supposed to be fun, like theater, usually bringing joy to casts and audiences alike. According to the information he had been given, however, this kind of *Drama* was not fun and was created to take the "joy out of living."

When *Drama* showed up for the meeting, she was wearing one of the most outrageous outfits *Joy* had ever seen. She captured a great deal of attention, though if someone ignored her for a moment, she would do something to make sure she recaptured it.

Joy had chosen to meet in the park. It was a beautiful day for an outdoor meeting. Listening to *Drama*, one would think it was an awful day as she complained that it was just a little too hot. "Oh, oh! This is just too much!" she exclaimed, as she cooled herself with a beautifully detailed folding fan that she had pulled from her handbag. *Joy* offered to move the meeting inside to a nearby ice cream parlor, but *Drama* then complained, "No, it would be far too cold in there. I can't take extreme temperature changes. They unsettle me so."

"I'll be glad to get you a soda," *Joy* offered.

Drama covered her face with her hands and rocked back and forth, wailing, "No, sodas are too sweet for my sensitive system."

"How about a cup of coffee, then?"

"Another extreme, my dear *Joy*," she answered, putting her hand up to her forehead. "Coffee is far too much of a stimulant for me. It makes me dizzy."

"Water, then?" *Joy* offered.

"Oh!" *Drama* snapped her little fan shut and tapped him lightly on the arm with it, saying: "Too boring."

Joy gave up. "Now I understand why I'm meeting with this little drama queen," he thought to himself. "Everything is such a big deal to her!"

"Okay, let's just get started then, Miss *Drama*," *Joy* said. "Tell me, what is your function for your clients?"

"What is my function? Oh my, are you sure you want to know?" *Drama* got up from the bench they were sitting on and made a grand, sweeping motion as she said, "I keep confusion going so that my clients don't get bored. They thrive on conflict, you see. My clients can take any situation at all and make a big deal out of nothing."

"*Drama*, why do your clients need confusion? Can't they exist with *Peace?*" *Joy* wondered aloud.

"Horrors, absolutely not!" she replied, clutching her throat. "My clients actually look for me, and I help them create drama so that people around my clients can't find you, *Joy.*"

He replied, "*Drama*, it sounds like your life is full of exciting scenes. Can you tell me about the ones that are the most exciting?

Drama thought for a moment, then answered, "That's hard; there are so many." She sat back down and placed her head in her hands while she thought about it. *Joy* looked on, amused.

Then *Drama* continued, "It's always exciting to see the drama playing out in families, especially between parents and teenagers. Everyone seems to get involved in those performances: you know, such as the teenage girl who throws a temper tantrum when she isn't allowed to date too soon; or the teenage boy who takes the family car out joy riding with his buddies, without permission.

"I am invited almost everywhere, but when my clients decide they want calm and peace instead, I leave. There are times when you can hear my clients yelling out loud, "Please, no more drama!" When I hear this, I know I am doing a good job. Of course, I enjoy my job tremendously. I get to perform in life's theaters in just about every arena. I can be found in the privacy of marriage, or I can show up at choir rehearsal at a local church. I once created drama in the simple matter of choosing a home for one of my clients. I have also been known to show up at high schools and colleges. Drama is what I do, and drama is what I like."

Now *Drama* got up from the bench again and performed a flourishing bow, pleased with her script. *Joy* just looked at her and was about to say something when suddenly she looked around and said, "You'll have to excuse me now. I see an opening over there for some drama."

"Where"? *Joy* wanted to know, as he gazed about.

"Over there, where those guys are playing ball. It appears that I have some potential clients on the diamond," *Drama* replied.

"Fine, *Drama*," *Joy* said. "But before you go, I want to know quickly what you think could prevent drama in the lives of your clients? *Drama* paused, and she thought about trying to create serious drama with *Joy*. Instead, she answered, "I hate to admit it, but if my clients realized that a soft answer will turn away wrath, much of the drama they create could be prevented. I also find that when the *Joy Builder* called *Humor* shows up, it really tones down the drama. Enough already, Mr. *Joy*. I must go now to create more theatrics."

Joy, always the gentleman, stood up as she prepared to leave and said, "I want you to know that I intend to replace you. Unfortunately, I don't think I can do it on my own, so I'll talk to my good friend *Peace*, and together I think we can bring a whole new life for your clients."

Laughing, tucking tendrils of hair under her hat as she prepared to head over to the softball diamond, *Drama* replied, "Whatever. It sounds really boring to me and I don't want any part of this plan."

To which *Joy* replied, "That's the idea, my dear *Drama*. You are not part of the plan."

Drama shrugged and walked off, chiming the sarcastic social sign-off of "See ya, wouldn't want to be ya!"

"You'd better start practicing your farewell song, Miss *Drama*," *Joy* retorted, "because that's what you'll be singing when I show up again with my buddy *Peace*!"

38

Joy Meets *Peace*

The seed of joy grows best in a field of peace.
—*Robert J. Wicks*

*P*eace had been a phenomenal mentor to *Joy*, and *Joy* always looked forward to spending time with him. Being with *Peace*, *Joy* thought to himself, is like hearing the "quiet whisper of a beautiful spring day." It was a calming presence that *Peace* always brought with him, and it captured all that was good and perfect. It was the stillness and quiet of knowing all is well. Whenever *Peace* entered a room, his every movement brought comfort. He always made *Joy* want to stay there forever.

Joy was aware that much of what he wanted to know from *Peace* would not come through his normal interviewing process. *Joy* understood that in order to understand *Peace*, he must learn to be comfortable with silence. He understood that *Peace* would create quiet space between his thoughts.

Joy had planned to interview *Peace* right after his earlier visit with *Purpose*, since they lived next door to one another. But *Peace* hadn't been at home, so *Joy* had gone on to the next interviewee, *Arrogance*. Now, however, he was certain *Peace* was in.

Joy walked up the quiet garden pathway at Peace Haven and rang the doorbell. *Peace* answered almost immediately. *Joy* was surprised to see that *Peace* appeared to have been roughed up a bit.

"Hey, there you are! I've been looking for you! What happened to you, *Peace?* Why do you have all those bruises?" *Joy* asked.

"I've been at a war zone, trying to negotiate a peace settlement," replied *Peace.* "Things got a little rough, especially when *Hatred* and *Anger* showed up and kidnapped me, but I finally prevailed, as I usually do when warring parties realize the only other options for them are *Death, Annihilation,* and no future.

"But I know you're not here to discuss the politics of peace," he continued. "You want to know about the gifts I give, inner peace and the quietness of your soul as you connect with God, am I right?"

"Yes, *Peace,* you are," *Joy* replied. "I'm here to find out more about the nature of your function and what we can do to create a stronger partnership to serve our clients."

"Well, then, come on in and have a seat, *Joy,* and we'll begin," said *Peace.* They walked into his living room and sat. Minutes passed. *Joy* and *Peace* just sat still, both focused on connecting to their source.

Peace began to whisper quietly, "Be still and know that I am God."

Joy understood exactly what was happening. *Peace* began talking, almost in a whisper. "My clients must know that I will surpass their understanding. There's not a place I won't go if my clients choose to take me. I have been in the middle of storms, and I have lived through excruciating pain, but I am always available to my clients. I am the emotion my clients can feel when they have experienced and then accepted the loss of a loved one. I can be that emotion that exudes calmness in spite of the disappointment and the sense of loss. I am the manifestation of mental, emotional, and spiritual balance."

Joy sat there motionless, meditating on the words *Peace* was saying, writing in his notebook when he could.

"My clients must fight the noise," *Peace* continued. "They can't be terrified of silence. They must learn to embrace it. One of my clients, Mother Teresa, expressed it best when she said 'God is a friend of silence.' See how nature—trees, grass—grow in silence; see the stars, the moon and the sun, how they move in silence.

"It's true," *Peace* continued, "that my clients will often be best served when they can arrange a time to be alone with God and their thoughts. My clients must always protect their peace and follow it when they make decisions. I am always there, but I can be destroyed only when I am ignored. My clients understand how to connect with their source and reduce their stress and tension. They understand that God is the source of their contentment, and their search for contentment will not take them to empty places."

Joy took a deep breath, absorbing all that *Peace* had shared. He felt content, as if he had received a gentle, soothing massage over his entire being. He was ready for the journey that was ahead, and he knew that *Peace* would continually draw him in with his clients.

"Whenever I spend time with you, I never want to leave," *Joy* said quietly to *Peace*.

"And I never want to leave the places I go, either," replied *Peace*, "but sometimes they kick me out, take my passport, and accuse me of causing trouble, can you imagine? They don't believe me when I say 'I come in peace.' Very disheartening, you know!"

"Incredible!" *Joy* responded. "However, you must know I am always so pleased on the occasions when you do prevail. I know that besides getting kicked out of warring countries, you also get kicked out of families, businesses, and individuals' minds, right?" *Joy* commented.

"Yes, that too," *Peace* replied, laughing gently, "only it's so funny because people always turn around and clamor that they want some 'peace and quiet around here.' Usually this happens when they feel tense about something, or when *Anger, Anxiety, Hatred, Drama,* and some of that other cast of characters show up."

Joy, who was feeling positively, wonderfully, and incredibly good, was stretching out on the floor as he continued the conversation. "When those *Joy Robbers* show up, *Peace*, you should call on me immediately to come help you out, as together we can probably run them off faster," he said.

Peace began to reply, but a thundering, cracking explosion drowned out the sound of his voice. *Joy*, startled, jumped to his feet and they both went running for cover as fast as their legs could take them. "What is going on here?" *Joy* shouted to him over the rumbling din. "Where is all this racket coming from?"

"It's the noise and debris from *Anxiety*, who is *Worry's* adopted sister, and she usually blusters in from everywhere!" *Peace* shouted back, as he dodged an errant set of office supplies that flew by in the explosion. "What you are witnessing is a World Anxiety Moment!"

"What? What is that? I've never heard of a World Anxiety Moment!"

"It's the name I've given to these special moments when *Anxiety* almost succeeds in taking over. But she does this only in short spurts. Our clients need to learn how to handle *Anxiety* when she decides to show up. Once her moment is over, well, it's over until the next time she finds an emotional opening.

"Of course, *Fear* rides along on the edge of her commotion, and *Worry* likes to be nearby, too, just in case! *Anxiety* drives everyone crazy when she causes these momentary flashes of disturbance in our clients' minds.

"Sometimes," *Peace* mused, "I wonder why when you met with *Worry,* she told you that she was so afraid that her clients would meet me. With her sister *Anxiety* and the shadow of *Fear* darkening every corner, *Worry* is pretty well protected, wouldn't you say?"

"I think it's our clients protecting *Worry* sometimes," *Joy* replied as he ducked a sailing wedding cake. "But what are some examples of the temporary disturbances that bring on these storm flashes from *Anxiety*?"

"An example just flew by right now," *Peace* responded. "That's all the brides in the world getting the jitters over their wedding day plans!"

"Wow! I had no idea brides get that nervous about their weddings! What else?" hollered *Joy*, as they continued running away from the disturbing racket.

"Well, there's all the high school seniors taking their college entrance exams, for one. How about all the law school students taking the bar exams, and medical students taking their exams? We have guys sweating it out because they want to ask a beautiful girl out on a first date. They are so afraid of being rejected. We have project managers trying to manage projects that have grown out of control, writers about to miss their deadlines, surgeons getting the shakes, engineers whose computers are crashing…"

"Watch out for that flying fiddle!" *Joy* warned, pushing *Peace* out of the way. "I guess the musicians of the world are playing sour notes and missing the beat today."

Back steady on his feet now, *Peace* continued giving examples. "We also have all the new job candidates going on their interviews, today, *Joy*. And speaking of new job candidates, we also have the new hires who are going in for their first day of work."

"Oh, yes," responded *Joy*. "I've heard that when a hurricane comes, newly hired meteorologists are expected to run out and tie themselves to a tree so they can make a first-person report to their television audiences!" *Joy* and *Peace* both tried not to laugh at this, but they couldn't help it.

"And here are examples that almost every parent has experienced," *Peace* said. "*Anxiety* is at her best with these! Mom is at the mall with her toddler, and the sweet little tyke gets away from her, heading straight for the escalator! Or Dad is at a crowded bus stop with Junior. He helps Junior get on, but in the meantime, the driver becomes distracted by someone asking for change. The driver shuts the door and the bus takes off, with Junior wailing and Dad running the marathon of his life! *Anxiety* has that one branded! It happens on trains sometimes, too."

The commotion seemed to be receding. Or maybe they had run far enough away from it. All was becoming quiet, and now only a soft, sweet breeze wafted the air. *Peace* gazed upward at a shimmering blue sky and said: "You know, sometimes our clients just need to sleep on whatever it is that's troubling them. When I can see that they've calmed themselves, I am very often able to leave them with the gift of the problem resolved or the solution found."

"*Peace*, you are really such an easygoing fellow to be with. I just can't figure out why more people don't take the time to get to know you," remarked *Joy*.

167

"Some of my clients just seem to prefer what they think of as 'acceptable drama' in their lives, I suppose. But I will always be available to anyone who wants to restore their spirits and their inner connection to God."

Later that day as *Joy* moved on quietly to his next assignment, he knew he would never say "goodbye" to *Peace*, never ask him to leave, never confiscate his passport.

39

Joy Meets *Control*

People are usually more convinced by reasons they discovered
themselves than by those found by others.
— *Blaise Pascal*

When *Joy* called *Control* to arrange a meeting, he found it
interesting that she would not meet with him unless she made
all of the arrangements. *Control* made it clear to *Joy* that the meeting
had to be under her terms. *Joy* was flexible about this, but at the same
time cautious, as it seemed this *Joy Robber* was a schemer.

Control had scheduled the meeting at her home, and with the
time set, she requested to start precisely on time, warning *Joy* not
to be late. *Joy* arrived on time and ready to find out all he could
about *Control*.

Control answered the door appearing a little uptight. Her greeting
sounded rather stiff as she told *Joy* to come in and make himself at
home. "But don't get too comfortable!" she warned. Even if he had
wanted to make himself feel at home, *Joy* knew he could not feel
totally at ease here. It certainly was not like being at *Love's* home or
Positive Attitude's home, where he had felt relaxed and
unconditionally welcomed.

Joy decided to get to the interview and began by asking *Control*
about her function for her clients.

"I help my clients exercise authority or influence over everything and everybody, including each other," *Control* began explaining. "My clients have to be the regulators over all situations. Just about everyone is a client, you know, because most people have control issues."

"Is this a good thing?" *Joy* jumped in and asked.

"Did I tell you that you could interrupt and ask me questions?" *Control* demanded.

"In a way, yes you did," *Joy* replied. "Interrupting you is a way for you to exhibit your controlling personality."

"Oh," *Control* responded. She wasn't sure if this was a compliment or not.

"Anyway, as I was saying," *Control* continued, "having control issues and this being a good or bad thing is a matter of perspective. Having a sense of control can be good for my clients' overall emotional health. However, when I roll out with the control freaks, you can usually recognize their characteristics. They are overly anxious, perfectionists, overly critical or demanding, very opinionated, close-minded, and they may have trouble delegating tasks. You will also recognize a control freak as the one who always has to win an argument."

Joy shook his head and replied, "This sounds rather complicated. On the one hand, your clients need you for some healthy thinking. And on the other hand, you produce an excess of control."

Control smiled. "Let me simplify this for you," she told *Joy*. "Keep in mind that no one wants to be controlled. That is the simple bottom line for all of my clients. While they themselves may be the controllers, they are like the rest of the world, and they don't like being controlled."

Control continued passionately, "You know that old saying, don't you? 'A man convinced against his will is of the same opinion still.' At the end of the day, *Joy*, life is still about choices, even when you are choosing to be manipulated and controlled.

Wondering how he could work with *Control*, *Joy* asked, "Do you think your clients need me?"

Looking as if *Joy* had just asked a stupid question, *Control* replied, "Of course. My clients don't always know they are controlling, and they need help to look at themselves without blaming themselves. They need you, *Joy*, to make the change. All of my clients must understand the difference between *Control* and *Order*. Sometimes they confuse the two."

"That's interesting," *Joy* commented. "Tell me what the difference is, because right now I'm not sure."

"If my clients have been given the responsibility to be in charge of a situation, company, or institution, they have been given the responsibility for *Order*. This doesn't give them license to *Control* people, because then they will have to violate *Choice* and *Personal Will*. And by the same token, people who report to my clients must understand that if you do not submit to *Order*, you will not be protected," *Control* answered.

"Protected?" asked *Joy*. "From what?"

Control almost smiled, saying: "You're interrupting without my permission again, but I'll explain further anyway. When my clients stop at a red light while driving, they are not controlled by the red light; they are submitting to *Order* so that they don't get into an accident. Sometimes people are confused by this and refuse to submit to authority because they feel they are being controlled. We all need someone in our life who can be our stoplight that brings order to life's traffic flow. When people don't recognize these legitimate stoplights, they can become involved in unnecessary accidents. Do you get what I mean *Joy*?"

Joy felt overwhelmed; he had learned more about *Control* than he ever wanted to know. *Control* certainly had proficient job knowledge; she knew all the angles. "You've made things very clear for me," he replied, "and I know now what I need to do to work with your clients. I will need to get your clients away from *False Joy*. Once your clients experience *True Joy*, I don't think they'll have the need to control anyone but themselves."

"All right, I'll send you my client list complete with their needs, and then you can get back to me with your specific plans." *Control* started telling *Joy.*

Interrupting again, *Joy* told her she was doing too much. "Let me remind you that now that we'll be working more closely, your life will be different for you and your clients. You don't need to be perfect or lead a micromanaged life for *Joy* to operate."

She smiled at *Joy* again, a real smile this time, recognizing that he was telling her the truth. "You know, after today I don't think I will be sweating the small stuff anymore," she said.

40

Joy Meets *Power*

Nearly all men can stand adversity, but if you want to
test a man's character, give him power.
— *Abraham Lincoln*

From the moment that *Joy* heard *Power* speak, he knew that this
was going to be an important meeting. *Joy* had arranged the
meeting with *Power* at the recommendation of *Control*, who had called
him with the suggestion after he left her house. *Control* mentioned
that she was always trying to get more of what *Power* had to offer for
her clients; however, at times rather than gaining real *Power*, her clients
became more insecure. *Control* had explained to *Joy* that her clients
compensate for a lack of power by using intimidating behavior or
micromanaging every aspect of thought, life, or work of the people
around them. *Joy* reflected on this post-meeting conversation with
Control as he entered the room.

Power, standing tall and speaking with a booming voice said, "*Joy*,
I'm so glad to see you! The word is out, so I know why you're here.
I have one of the most enviable client lists around. I'm sure you know
my clients as the movers and the shakers of the world. They're among
the world's most influential people; however, you shouldn't make
the mistake of confusing influence with position."

Joy nodded as if he understood but then said, "Will you clarify that for me, please?"

"Of course. Many of my clients have the power of influence," *Power* explained, "although they may not have the title or the position that people expect. For example, *Joy*, among my most powerful clients are homemakers, receptionists, and personal assistants. They may not hold top-level positions, but they understand that they have powerful influence, and they use that power wisely. On the other side of the coin, I have clients who have gained power by making it to powerful positions, such as head of state or CEO of a company."

"Can you tell me if power is a good thing or a bad thing, then?" *Joy* asked, fascinated by *Power's* wisdom.

"Power can be used with grace and generosity for universal benefit by individuals who possess a solid sense of security and self-esteem," was the reply. "On the other hand, power can be misused with *Abuse, Arrogance,* and *Selfishness* by insecure people."

"So where do your clients find you?" *Joy* asked next.

"They inherit me, buy me or earn me. However," *Power* continued, "if power isn't earned, it rarely remains. *Joy*, I must make a distinction here, because there is a power that no mortal can truly possess, and that is 'all power in both heaven and earth.'"

"Why wouldn't mortals be able to possess that kind of power?" *Joy* asked.

"Because then they wouldn't be mortals," was *Power's* short reply. Continuing, he said, "All power in heaven and earth belongs to God."

Joy's fascination with *Power* was growing; he had so much to offer! "What can I bring to your clients, *Power*?" he asked.

Power paused, giving the question some thought. "You, *Joy*, can cause my clients to experience you, which will in turn cause them to make sure others experience you. My clients have the power to bring about change, so you can make sure they experience the change that they have the power to bring about."

Joy smiled, beginning to feel powerful himself, talking about what could happen with their partnership. *Power* smiled, too. "Let's have an arm wrestling contest, *Joy*," he proposed. "The winner's entitled to bragging rights. How about it?"

Joy immediately accepted this challenge, more out of surprise than anything. It seemed to have come from out of the blue, and he wondered if he really had the physical strength to take on *Power*. But then, he reasoned quickly to himself, this could be an important contest for him if he were able to say he defeated *Power*.

The arm wrestling contest began. It looked like *Joy* was doomed from the start. *Power* began exerting strength. *Joy* grimaced with his own exertion, but shook and gasped as he lost control. Then *Joy* began to think about his own mental *Power*. Recalling his conversation with *Positive Attitude*, he thought, "If I don't have the physical strength, I'd better have the mental strength." In that moment, *Joy* began to concentrate, his mind directed to the focus, energy, and strength required to win this challenge. Not long after, *Power* found his arm face down on the table.

"Congratulations, *Joy*!" *Power* exclaimed. "You would have lost the contest if you had not discovered the *Power* of the mind."

"You're right," *Joy* agreed. "I have just learned a powerful lesson."

41

Joy Meets *The Future*

Never be afraid to trust an unknown future
to a known God.
— *Corrie ten Boom*

It was time to review his notes again. As he looked them over, *Joy* realized that he had put together the first draft of an extensive evaluation of the *Joy Robbers* and the *Joy Builders*. With what he had learned, he felt newly empowered to do much more to bring joy to his clients. He felt energized as he realized he could renew and expand his joy operation to many more people.

Despite life's challenges, *Joy* was certain now that he could be the gatekeeper for consistent joy, and that when people found this joy, they would also find renewed strength. This was his purpose, he knew now, and fulfilling it for others was fulfilling it for himself. *Joy* was excited about all he had learned. Some information was a bit scary, he thought, but he also knew that lack of knowledge could destroy everything he had worked for. So he headed toward the future to make sure that he would always have a place there. This would be his last meeting, but it was a critical meeting for himself and *The Future*.

They shook hands, and *Joy* told *The Future* how pleased he was to meet him, since he had heard so much about him. "Likewise!" *The Future* replied appreciatively to *Joy*.

"I've been on an extensive journey to understand the *Joy Robbers* and *Joy Builders*," *Joy* began explaining. He continued, "My plan is to ensure that no one steals joy from my clients. I've learned a lot and am prepared now to continue my work." Pausing to study *The Future's* face for his reaction, he then continued, "How can I ensure a place with you?"

The Future replied, "*Joy*, the three things your clients must remember to do are:
- Learn from the past
- Live in the present
- Prepare for the future.

He continued, adding, "The future is not meant to be a mystery. If you have learned from the mistakes of the past and you are living fulfilled in the present, the future is simply an extension of those elements."

"I never thought of it that way!" *Joy* exclaimed. "But aren't there going to be elements of *The Future* that my clients will never know?"

Nodding his head, *The Future* replied, "Absolutely. The part of the future you do not know is the part that you do not control. The best way to get to know the parts you do not control is to know 'The One' who has those answers. Keep in mind that knowing someone who has answers is not the same as knowing God, Who has all answers."

Joy waited a moment to give himself time to absorb and really think about what was said, because he knew that he had to make his clients understand this point clearly. "Do you think my clients can take their current joy and bring it with them into their futures?" he asked.

"That depends on whether your clients want to experience just a pleasant life or if they desire true happiness," *The Future* replied. "Your clients can leave in the past their failures, their disappointments, their sadness, and even some of their successes; however, for true happiness, they will want to bring their joy into the future, because that's what will keep it bright."

"If I were one of my own clients," *Joy* replied, "I think I would definitely choose true happiness over just a pleasant life." Smiling, he pulled out a pair of sunshades and put them on.

"*Joy,* what are you doing with those shades on? Are you getting ready for Hollywood?" *The Future* asked, laughing.

"Nope," replied *Joy*, laughing back. "I'm preparing for my future, because it's so bright that I have to wear shades as I approach it."

"That's the right attitude, *Joy*," *The Future* answered, adding, "You will possess what you continually confess!"

As *Joy* continued on his journey into the future, he remembered the commitment his boss had made to all of his clients. His boss had made it clear that the plans he had for them were good. He had reminded them that the plan is to give them *Hope* and a *Future. Joy* had memorized this statement because it was important to move forward. *Joy* knew that he could not stay in the future, because he had lots of work in the present. He was glad that he had visited *The Future*, because as he went back to the present, he could give his clients a lot of reasons to keep him around.

42

Joy's Final Meeting

Man's business here is to know for the sake of living,
not to live for the sake of knowing.
—*Frederic Harrison*

In my dream, *Joy* left *The Future*, and I encountered him once again. I was very excited to see him and asked him about his journey. *Joy* replied that it was very successful, and he had learned a lot. He thought aloud, "I have so much information!"

"What are your plans to be victorious?" I asked him.

He replied, "I have the list of the *Joy Robbers'* clients." Looking at me intently, *Joy* continued, "My plan to ensure my victory is to give these clients all the information I got from talking to the *Joy Robbers*. I don't want anyone to be destroyed or lose their joy because they lack knowledge.

"I'm going to let these clients know exactly what the *Joy Robbers* are doing to ruin their lives, and let them know what is available from the *Joy Builders* to find true joy and true happiness. I have a press release that's ready to go out immediately. I also plan to email their hearts, so that they don't only think and evaluate change, but also feel the emotional need for change."

I was excited to hear of *Joy's* plans, but then I thought, "*Joy*, what if people can't make the change, then what? I thought the whole point of this journey is that you would find ways to rescue all of us from the *Joy Robbers.*"

He must have understood my question at a very deep level. *Joy* smiled at me and said, "I must tell you a story that I heard during my journey. I think it will answer your questions.

"Once there was this wise old man who lived in a thriving neighborhood. He was so wise that everyone wondered how and why he always seemed to have the right answer. The teenagers in the neighborhood decided to outsmart the wise man. They decided among themselves that they would approach the wise man and tell him that they had a bird in their hands. They would ask the wise man if the bird were dead or alive. If the wise man said the bird was alive, they were going to smother the bird so that the bird would die, and the wise man would be wrong. If the wise man said the bird was dead, they would simply open their hands let the bird fly away, and the wise man would be wrong. This way, however the wise man answered, he would be wrong.

"The teenagers approached the wise man and asked, 'Tell us, Mr. Wise Man, is the bird in our hands dead or alive?'

"The wise man looked into the eyes of each of the teenagers and replied, 'Young people, the bird is in your hands, so it is whatever you want it to be,' and then he walked away."

I listened silently as *Joy* continued, "Every day people wake up and make a decision about what they hold in their hands. They can be holding the effects of the *Joy Robbers* or the effects of authentic *Joy*. Each day, every person must make the call about what is in their hands. I realize that I can't rescue anyone, but my clients always have the power to rescue themselves.

"At the end of the day, my clients decide whether I go or stay. Through this journey, I've learned the limitations of my power and the greatness of the power my clients possess. They make the decisions, and I simply obey."

As my dream ended, I saw a bright blue sky pierced by the jewel-like colors of a beautiful rainbow, the sun its shimmering backdrop. The golden orb seemed held in place by a feathery chain of soft, silver-streaked clouds as it glowed and dangled beneath the rainbow arch like a gilded, luminous pendant. This, indeed, was God's heavenly artwork.

I looked up and broke into an uncontrollable, radiant smile. Mesmerized by the beautiful rainbow and its fiery ornament, I looked around to tell *Joy* to see the splendor before us, but *Joy* had disappeared. He was gone. Then I remembered that earlier he had told me he would need to go back and meet with his boss. As my dream faded, I saw myself laughing out loud, and then I called out to *Joy* in his absence, "I've made my decision, *Joy.*" I woke up.

43

Joy Meets You

One joy scatters a hundred griefs.
— *Unknown*

Perhaps you identified "who stole your joy" as you read this book. It is never too late to get your joy back and keep it intact. Use your greatest *Joy Protectors*, which are the words that you speak. Make it a daily practice to affirm your joy. To get you started, here is your beginning affirmation. I wish you continued joyous living!

- Today, I choose to wake up with a smile and with joy in my heart.
- I choose to have a positive attitude, and I will stand tall with my purpose in mind.
- I will overcome the obstacles that stand in my way, because I "say it so."
- I can serve others and not lose my own identity.
- I believe in myself, in much laughter, and in ending well.
- I know with God all things are possible, and that my joy in Him is authentic and complete.

Inspiration

The Holy Bible, New International Version. Grand Rapids, MI: Zondervan, 1984.

Beard, Steven E. and Lee. *Wake up and Live the Life You Love.* Laguna Beach, CA: Little Seed Publishing, 2003.

Carlson, Richard. *Don't Sweat the Small Stuff . . . And It's All Small Stuff.* New York: Hyperion, 1997.

Carnegie, Dale. *How to Win Friends and Influence People.* New York: Pocket Books, 1981.

de la Rochefoucauld, François. Available from http://www.cybernation.com. Accessed May 19, 2004.

Jones, Laurie Beth. *Grow Something Besides Old—Seeds for a Joyful Life.* New York: Simon and Schuster, 1998.

Lucado, Max. *Grace for the Moment.* J. Countryman, a division of Thomas Nelson, 2001.

Maxwell, John. *The Power of Attitude.* Tulsa, OK: River Oak Publishing, 2001.

Mother Teresa. Available from http://www.inspirationpeak.com/life.html. Accessed 27 Apr. 2004.

Munroe, Myles. *Releasing Your Potential.* Shippensburg, PA: Destiny Image Publishers, 1992.

Olivier, Laurence. As quoted in *Simpson's Contemporary Quotations,* compiled by James B. Simpson. Publisher: Houghton Mifflin Company, 1988. Available from http://www.bartlesby.com/63/63/8963.html. Accessed 15 May 2004.

Peter, Dr. Laurence J. *Peter's Quotations: Ideas for Our Time.* New York: Bantam Books, 1987.

Seligman, Martin. *Authentic Happiness: Using the New Positive Psychology to Realize Your Potential for Lasting Fulfillment.* Free Press, 2002.

Taddeo, Daniel. *Notable Quotables: 3000 Quotations from A to Z.* Provo, UT: Creation House, 2003.

Warren, Rick. *The Purpose-Driven Life.* Grand Rapids, MI: Zondervan, 2002.

Wilson, P.B. *Knight in Shining Armor.* Eugene, OR: Harvest House, 1995.

Wilson, Tom and Tom II. *Ziggy.* Available from http://www.quoteland.com topic.asp?CATEGORY_ID=13. Accessed 15 May, 2004.

Acknowledgments

I would like to express my deep sense of gratitude to the following people who have each taught me important aspects of JOY.

Joan Harrington, who has shown me the joy of excellence through her unlimited creativity while editing this manuscript.

My mother, who showed me the joy of having faith until the end.

My grandmother, who showed me the joy of giving.

Aunt Mary, who has shown me the joy of wisdom.

Mother Campbell, who has shown me the joy of generosity.

Rick Godwin, who has shown me the joy of having relationship with God without the boundaries of religion.

Cindy Godwin, who has shown me the joy of friendship.

Max Lucado, who has shown me the joy of simplicity, power and humility.

Myles Munroe, who has shown me the joy of living a life of purpose.

Bunny Wilson, who has shown me the joy of meeting with God in the morning.

Amelia Hartzel, who has shown me the joy of genuine service.

Guy Morrell, who has shown me the joy of having a publisher who believes in the message.

To a host of **family and friends** who have taught me the joy of allowing LOVE to guide you.

Index

Who Stole My Joy? Characters